FIRST MOVES

FIRST MOVES

HOW TO START
A CHESS GAME

D B Pritchard

RIGHT WAY

Typeset in 11 on 12pt Times by
County Typesetters, Margate, Kent.

Made and printed in Great Britain by
Cox and Wyman Ltd., Reading, Berks.

The *Right Way* series and the *Paperfront* series are both
published by Elliot Right Way Books, Brighton Road,
Lower Kingswood, Tadworth, Surrey KT20 6TD. U.K.

FIRST MOVES

The aim of this book is to guide the novice (you, I suspect?) through the first stages of a game of chess, playing either as White or Black. No knowledge of chess, other than the rules, has been assumed.

These first moves for both sides are known as the Opening. The Openings have been formulated in part by analysis but mostly through play, usually between masters, though moves in play are often the fruits of prior research. Openings have names and each opening has variations and subvariations, many of which will also have names. If you start the game with a bad move, or respond with one, you will probably find that the opening is unnamed, in which case you can name it after yourself, but don't expect anyone else to notice.

A huge number of books have been written about the openings, and even about single openings or variations. These books are mostly intended for strong players and are not much use to you who have taken but two steps down the long road to mastery. Openings, in the formalised sense, refer to series of moves by both players that have been accepted as playable; that is, not leading to a serious disadvantage for either side. If we assume, and it is reasonable to do so, that the average opening extends from ten to twenty moves, then it can be appreciated that the number of playable lines in which neither player makes any big mistake is, for practical purposes, limitless.

Our knowledge of the openings is advancing all the time; new lines are explored, old lines revitalised, judgments made. On top of that, fashions change.

Do not be intimidated at the prospect: more than one world champion has been noted for his deficiencies in this stage of the game. A former British champion, whom we shall call X, was renowned for his lack of opening knowledge. One day he was playing Y, also a former British champion and an opening buff. X surprised Y with a move recommended by the Russians (who are rather good at chess) in analysis that had reached Y only a day or two previously. How could X have known about it? He had not: asked after the game, our opening cripple replied, 'I never seriously considered any other move.'

That points up the lesson that if you play according to sound principles, you are likely to follow the approved openings whether you know them or not.

This is not to decry opening knowledge. Other things being equal, the player who is better versed in the openings is at an advantage. However, parrot learning of opening moves (everyone deplores it; everyone does it) is to be avoided as far as possible, particularly at this undistinguished stage in your chess career. There is no merit in playing your first ten, carefully rehearsed, moves like Karpov or Kasparov if, on your eleventh move, your memory exhausted, you play like King Kong.

This is not to suggest that you are an ape, but first things come first. You are starting to play chess and the most important thing at the moment is to widen your familiarity with the game – its tactics, its strategy, how to attack and how to defend. And the openings are a good place to begin.

Common advice to the beginner is to concentrate on one or two openings and learn these well. The argument runs that you have only limited time to devote to the game, that this way you will gain confidence, and you will also achieve better results (you won't lose so quickly).

Forget it. You would be wise to reject the comfort of the familiar. That does not mean embracing the bizarre: it means experimenting with every type of opening. You will certainly meet catastrophe on occasion, but you will be learning more and more about chess, experience self-denied to the two-opening player.

You will by now realise that this book is not a conventional introduction to the chess openings and it may be as well to repeat here what was said at the beginning. This is a book to get you started. When you have finished it, as it is to be hoped you will, you will know very little about the openings. But you will have absorbed a number of useful principles, a lot of sound ideas, and you will have improved your game to the point where you can at least lick King Kong. And that is a good grounding for taking up a proper study of the openings. If you want to, that is. If not, then at least you will be equipped to handle the opening competently and have the experience to deal with new situations. That should give you the advantage over most casual players, who don't usually think constructively, and over most chess computers, which don't think at all.

You have had enough of being talked at for the moment so let's get down to the board. Hereon, you will find it useful to have a chess set in front of you, set up for play.

The diagrams in this book show the board either from White's or Black's standpoint, according to the idea under discussion. You should get used to looking at positions from both sides.

MOVE ONE

You know the starting position *(1)*

BLACK

WHITE

1

Unless you are familiar with chess diagrams you may confuse the king and queen, so here is a royal identity parade:

King ♔ ♚

Queen ♕ ♛

There is no known way in which one side can force an advantage. If there were, there would be no chess openings and probably no game called chess. This position is as baffling today as it has always been.

There are 20 possible opening moves for White. Of these, two are more popular than all the others combined. Most chess games, whether between modest players, experts or masters, are opened by moving up one of the central pawns, thus:

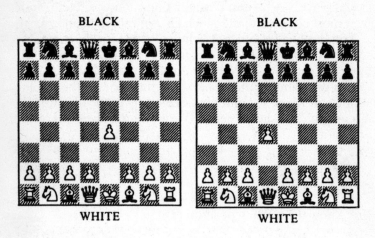

BLACK   BLACK

WHITE   WHITE

2   3

That does not mean that other moves are inferior. Here are two good opening moves that are by no means uncommon:

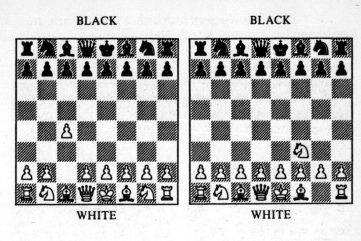

4   5

Certain other moves, though less often played, also have their merits. Here are two:

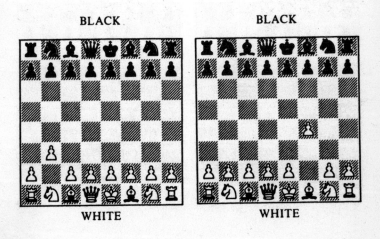

6   7

On the other hand, some opening moves are to be condemned as downright bad. Here are four:

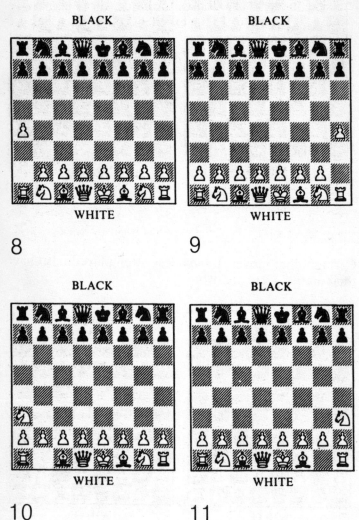

BLACK

WHITE

8

BLACK

WHITE

9

BLACK

WHITE

10

BLACK

WHITE

11

The first move of a chess game carries no threats. It follows that Black has a variety of options for his reply.

Again, some are recognized as better than others while some are simply more popular than others. Let us consider plausible responses to the usual opening moves *(2)* & *(3)*. In both cases, an excellent course for Black is to respond in the same way:

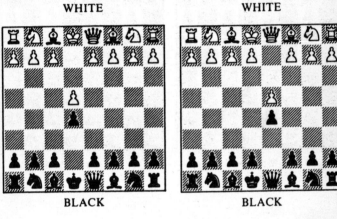

12   13

Other good responses to *(2)* are the following:

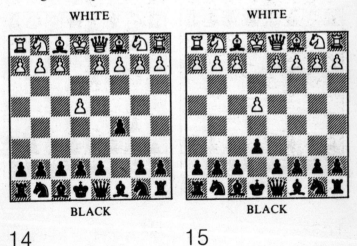

14   15

Several others are perfectly playable:

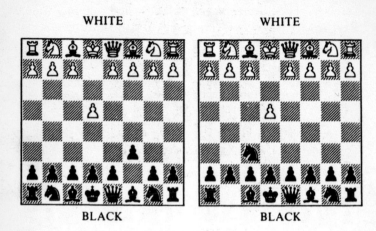

16

17

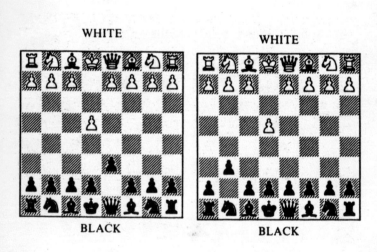

18

19

20

Other good responses to *(3)* are:

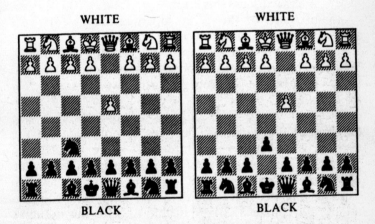

21 **22**

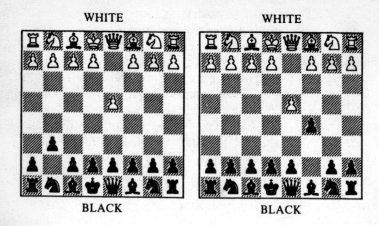

23   **24**

Notice that in *(24)* Black immediately offers a pawn to be taken. We will discuss this later.

Against each of the White opening moves *(4)* – *(7)* above, Black also has a choice of good responses.

However White opens, and however Black responds, White on his second turn will again have a choice of good moves. But before we progress further we must pause for a bit of theory.

The first move is a definite advantage. This fact determines the general objectives of both sides in the early stages of a game: White must strive to keep the advantage and must therefore play aggressively while Black will be seeking equality and will need to establish a cautious balance between defensive play and counter-attack. Of course, if Black is able to seize the initiative because of weak play by White, he will forget about equality and go over to the offensive.

Experts disagree about chess openings as experts are wont to disagree about everything. Nevertheless, certain strategic principles are not disputed, and of these two are paramount:

(i)   Get your pieces into play as soon as possible

(ii) Direct your play towards the centre of the board

Developing your pieces ('developing' is the jargon word) means placing them on squares where they are effective for attack or defence and preferably both. In the starting position, the only pieces (as distinct from pawns) that can move are the knights. It is necessary to move at least two pawns before you can develop all the other pieces. What are the problems of development? Two, principally: your own pawns, which have a habit of getting in the way, and your opponent, who is not enthusiastic about your pieces occupying strong points and is likely to take such measures as he is able to stop them doing so.

Why direct your play towards the centre, and what is the centre anyway? The centre is important because it confers flexibility. A piece at the side of the board usually commands less squares than one in the centre and cannot be moved so easily to other parts of the board. It is therefore less effective.

The centre can be defined as the four central squares and, loosely, the twelve squares immediately around them *(25)*

25

Let us now look at the moves above *(2)* – *(24)* in the light of these cardinal principles.

Moves (2) and (3) are admirable. They occupy central squares and at the same time allow bishop and queen to develop. Move (4) also strikes at the centre and frees the queen. Move (5) is a developing move, placing the knight on an ideal square to influence the central battle.

Notice that it is the king's knight (the knight on the king's side of the board). There is a good reason for this. The move assists preparation for castling on the king's side. The king is vulnerable in the middle and another opening principle is that he should be moved to safety before the main battle. This usually means castling, whereby a rook is simultaneously brought into play. Castling is both a protective and a developing move.

Castling on the king's side is favoured, for two reasons: it is easier to accomplish (one less piece to move out of the way) and, after castling, the rook's pawn (the pawn at the edge of the board) is guarded by the king, which it is not when castling queen's side.

Move (6) is harder to understand. It forms a redoubt for the bishop which will advance to the square vacated by the pawn. Here the piece will strike at the centre, protected from pawn attack. Thus the move meets our two criteria, if indirectly. It is therefore rather passive.

That is not to condemn it: it is part of an opening system. A system is a co-ordinated series of moves governed by strategic ideas. Development should not be at random but part of a general plan in which the pawns and pieces not only work to achieve their objectives, but also co-operate with and complement one another. There is nothing complex about this: all received openings are systems and these systems are likely to have long-term goals, like attacking on the king's side, securing the better pawn formation, exchanging off a powerful enemy bishop, and so forth. Do not let these trouble you at present.

Move (7) is a reflection of move (4) but carries a small element of risk since it opens lines near the king. Notice that if White had advanced this pawn only one square, the move would be thoroughly bad since it would carry the same element of risk but would not hit at the centre and would take away the best square for development of the knight.

It should now be clear why moves *(8)* – *(11)* are bad. They do not influence the centre and, in the case of *(10)* and *(11)*, the knights are badly placed for both attack and defence. Beginners sometimes favour *(8)* and *(9)* as the simplest way of getting the rooks into play. This idea is mistaken; rooks do not belong in front of pawns where they are very vulnerable to attack.

Black's responses to White's opening moves need not detain us long.

It should be obvious why *(12)*, *(13)* and *(14)* are good. Move *(15)* appears passive – although it releases one bishop, it shuts the door on the second one – but again this is the case of a system, which we will examine later.

Recall that Black must be careful in the early stages and this cautious approach is also reflected in *(16)* and *(18)*. Move *(20)* on the other hand is instant aggression and although it is quite playable, it is not a favourite of the experts. You can probably deduce why.

The other Black replies need no comment, and you should not be in need of any more horrid examples – you can work out a few defective Black responses for yourself.

A CAUTIONARY INTERLUDE

We will now return to the board for a minute or two to look at a couple of ideas.

Suppose that after the opening moves *(20)* White decides to develop his bishop and at the same time give check *(26)*. Is this a good idea? It is not. Checks are sometimes useful, sometimes useless. This one is rather worse than useless. Black replies as in *(27)* and now White must move the bishop again as it is attacked.

Where can he move it to? If he doesn't want to lose the

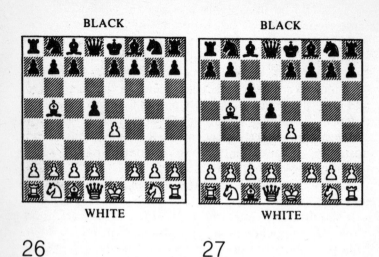

BLACK

BLACK

WHITE

WHITE

26   27

pawn (pawns are valuable and should not be surrendered lightly, particularly pawns in the centre), he must play as in *(28)*. Notice how the bishop's role is now reduced to that of a pawn, and further, the piece blocks the advance of the queen's pawn, adding to White's problems.

You may argue that Black's second move took away the best square from his knight even though it opened a line for the queen. Quite true, but in chess, as in life, it is rare to get something for nothing – be content, as Black would be here, that you are getting the better of the bargain.

Black seizes the centre by occupation *(29)* – notice that both his bishops are thereby released into play.

How is White to continue? Logically, he will want to get his king's knight developed sooner rather than later since he will be anxious to get his king to safety – it would take him at least four moves before he could think about castling on the queen's side.

So he tries *(30)*, which attacks a pawn. Black now forces the win of bishop or knight for pawn with the sequence shown in *(31) – (35)*. This pawn fork of two minor pieces is

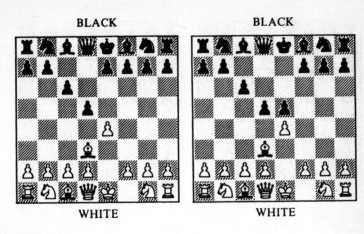

28   29

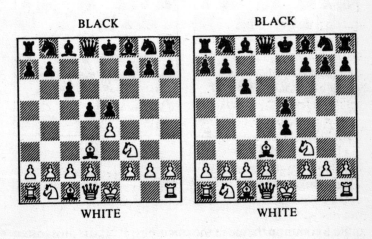

30   31

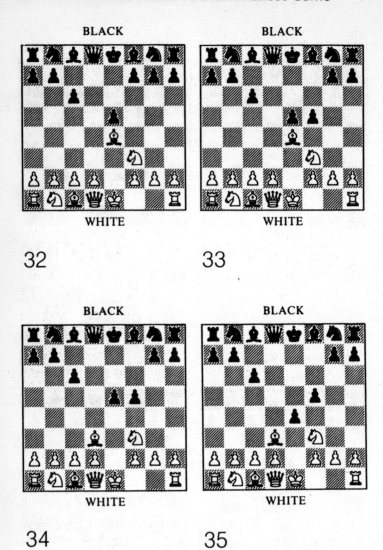

BLACK

WHITE

32

BLACK

WHITE

33

BLACK

WHITE

34

BLACK

WHITE

35

quite a common theme in the openings. It occurs most often in the middle of the board. Be on your guard against it!

Another idea for White: why not exploit the advantage

of the first move by bringing out the queen – the most powerful piece on the board – to bludgeon the black king? This manoeuvre is the novice's delight, the curtain-raiser of untold billions of games, but please reserve your applause.

Following from *(12)* (page 11), White develops a bishop where it bears down on Black's king position at the same time assisting preparations for castling *(36)*. A good idea? Certainly: faultless play so far.

Black responds, let us say (since he has other satisfactory moves), as in *(37)*, a sound developing play.

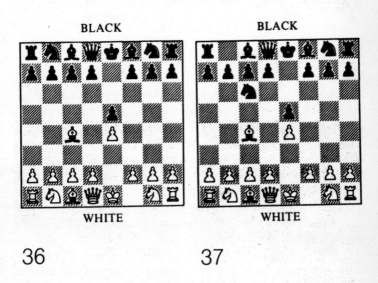

36   **37**

Now White advances his queen, threatening to checkmate Black *(38)*. Black easily parries the threat *(39)* when the position of White's queen proves something of an embarrassment. It is occupying the square wanted for the king's knight and may later be attacked with advantage by the enemy queen's knight or, after Black moves his queen's pawn, by the bishop. Black has the initiative.

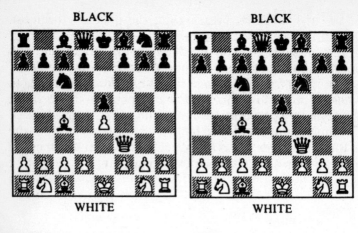

BLACK

BLACK

WHITE

WHITE

38   39

What have we learnt from these abortive ideas? A lesson that is valid for all opening play. Avoid attacks where the defence has an adequate resource and your pieces can be driven back with loss of time, or where they are left stranded on bad squares from which they must be moved, again with loss of time. Attacking moves with the queen in the opening sometimes work; but mostly they don't. The queen is best left indoors for a bit since she is particularly vulnerable to attack. The time to bring the queen out is when there are weaknesses in the enemy position of which advantage can be taken.

It is tempting to make attacking moves that depend on your opponent overlooking an obvious threat and in this way you may sometimes win games. If that pleases you, go ahead, but don't waste time reading further – this book is about improving your chess.

NOTATION

It is impossible to make much headway in studying chess without understanding notation which is a shorthand method of recording moves. It is necessary, therefore, to suspend our opening researches briefly so that we can progress faster later on.

The algebraic notation (there are others) is now the standard notation world-wide. The system uses initial letters to identify pieces, a few simple symbols to denote actions, like capturing, and a letter/number combination to identify squares. In this way any move can be recorded briefly and accurately.

Men
The initial N is commonly used for Knight to avoid confusion with King (K). Other piece initials (Q,R,B) cannot be confused. Pawns are not specifically identified, a pawn move being understood in default of an initial letter. Instead, the file on which a pawn stands immediately prior to a capture is sometimes given.

Actions

Symbol	Meaning
x	captures
+ (or) ch	check
0–0	castles king's side
0–0–0	castles queen's side
(Q) (or) (=Q)	promotion to queen
!	good move
?	bad move

Squares
Every square has a unique letter/number combination. Files (columns) are lettered a–h, left to right, from White's viewpoint, whilst ranks (rows) are numbered 1–8 from White's side. Thus White's nearest left-hand corner square

is a1; Black's equivalent being h8. Figures *40* and *41* should make this clear.

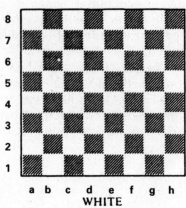

40

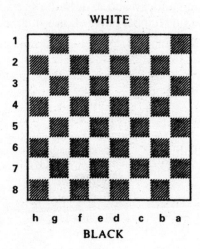

41

Moves

Notation, as we observed, is shorthand, so anything that is not essential is omitted from our move description. The formula is:

(1) Initial letter (if piece, but not pawn moved), (2) x (if capture involved), (3) identification of square to which move is made, (4) check/promotion/judgment if appropriate.

Thus a White move might be recorded as 27 exf8(Q)+! (White's 27th move is pawn on e7 takes opposing piece (not identified since there can be only one piece involved) on f8, promoting to queen and simultaneously giving check – a good move).

Return to figure *(12)* (page 11). The moves for both sides would be recorded as 1. e4 e5; the first move being White's and the second (Black's first move) Black's. Similarly *(13)* would be described as 1. d4 d5 and the moves in *(26)* (page 18) as 1 e4 d5 2 Bb5+ (only one of the white bishops can move to b5 so there is no need to state which one).

Sometimes ambiguity can arise however, when it is necessary to make clear which piece has been moved. This is done by indicating either the file or rank on which the piece is standing prior to the move. For example, supposing White plays a rook to e1 but both the white rooks, which let us say stand on a1 and f1, are able to move to that square. In this case it is necessary to record the move as Rae1 (if the rook on a1 is moved) or Rfe1. Similarly, if White has rooks on d1 and d7 and the rook on d7 is moved to d2, then, since Rd2 would be ambiguous, the move would be recorded as R7d2.

A final point: files a,b,c,d are commonly referred to as the Queen's side and files e,f,g,h as the King's side.

Now we can make use of notation to follow and discuss opening play.

PAWNS ARE IMPORTANT

Many chessplayers (though none who are any good) look on pawns as something of a nuisance, particularly in the opening where, as we have observed, they can get in the way of piece development. After all, isn't the object of the game to checkmate the enemy king? And doesn't that mean attacking with your pieces?

We have seen that pawns are moved in the opening for two main reasons; to allow the pieces to come into play and to contest the centre. Pawns have other uses, too. They are ideal to spearhead an attack and to serve as a shield in defence. Nor is that all. Squares attacked by your pawns are unlikely to find favour with your opponent as resting places for his pieces – nobody likes giving up a piece for a paltry pawn. And that leads to the idea of sometimes posting pawns specifically to inhibit enemy pieces from occupying strong posts. After the opening moves in *(2)* and *(3)* (page 8) for example, both sides attack two important squares in the centre.

From all of which you can see that pawns are extremely useful men. But they do have a weakness; they cannot retreat. That means that you have to be extra careful about advancing them. A charge with your pawns line abreast may be exhilarating and even intimidating, but it is unlikely to be sound.

Since pieces must give way to pawns as well as being blocked by them, the pawn structure, or skeleton as it is sometimes called, dominates the early stages of a game.

Let us forget the pieces for a moment and just look at a few pawn skeletons.

You will have little difficulty in identifying *(42)* as bad for Black, nor the reason for it: failure to contest the centre and a cramped position – the bishops have no choice of squares. Space confers flexibility and we shall consider this concept more fully later.

White's pawn structure in *42* is excellent. To establish safely pawns on d4 and e4 (or d5 and e5 in the case of Black) is an ideal that is often hard to achieve.

By contrast, *(43)* is good for both sides. White has occupied the centre and Black has contested it. White can advance his e-pawn further when Black will probably strike at its support with c5 and the position is about equal.

Notice that, if White allows it, Black would be able later to convert his weak pawn formation in *(42)* to the much more favourable formation in *(43)*. But that would mean moving the d-pawn a second time to attain a square that could have been reached in one move, which would be a loss

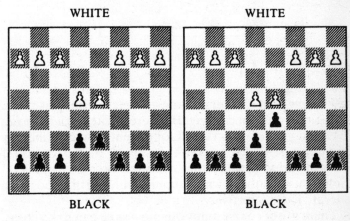

WHITE   WHITE

BLACK   BLACK

42   43

of time. Time is another important opening idea which we shall look at often. Loss of time is usually more serious for Black than for White because he is already handicapped by having to move second.

Now, how would you evaluate the pawn position in *(44)*?

There is not much in it. Black has occupied the best central squares but White's moves also strike at the centre which, because the pawn pairs attack each other, is unstable.

We have seen that moving the f-pawn early in the game exposes the white king to slight risks *(7)* (page 9). There can be danger of a queen check at h4 before castling and of a

BLACK

WHITE

44

bishop check at c5 after castling – indeed a bishop at c5 can sometimes prevent castling. But here White has a purpose: to exchange the f-pawn for the opponent's e-pawn, thereby opening the f-file. When White castles (0–0), the rook on f1 will be bearing down on the enemy position. So there is yet another use for the pawn – to unblock files so that rooks can operate more effectively.

There are of course many other possible pawn skeletons, which may be mobile, where one or more pawns are able to advance, or static, where the pawns are locked together. However the pawns are structured, they will strongly influence, if not dictate, the development of the pieces and the subsequent play. Make no bones about it – pawn skeletons are important!

TIME, PLEASE!

Suppose White opens 1. c4 *(4)* (page 9). Black could well respond with 1 . . . e5. Does this position *(45)* strike you as familiar? Look back at *(14)* (page 11) and you will see that it is identical – except for one thing; the colours are reversed.

So what is happening? Simply this: White is playing Black's defence but with the important difference that he has a move in hand.

There is no doubt that in chess, squares of alternating colour assist our perception of the board. As one early writer put it, 'the distinction of bicolored chequers is an elegant guide to the eye in diagonal movements'.

But the contrast can dazzle and sometimes blind. Did you notice at once the relationship between *(45)* and *(14)*?

BLACK

WHITE

45

It is helpful to look at openings, including those in this book, from both sides of the board. It is surprising how different the same position can appear and, more fruitfully, how the comparison can generate new ideas. (It is not uncommon for a master, when it is not his turn to play, to get up and look at the game from his opponent's angle.)

Another visual exercise that can be rewarding, though for less obvious reasons, is to view the board as black with a pattern of white squares superimposed, and then reverse the image. This can also lead to revelations. It is a fact that chequered squares, as well as assisting the unpracticed eye, can also beguile it into blunders by inflicting a temporary 'colour blindness'.

But back to the question of time which, as we have seen, when applied to the chessboard means moves, and not the time taken to make them.

One way to gain time is by giving up a pawn, or perhaps two, and rarely even a piece, to speed development. Such a sacrifice, commonly called a gambit, should not be undertaken lightly. Pawns, as we know, are like kruger-rands, to be surrendered only for adequate compensation. If the defender is able to repel the subsequent attack and hold on to his extra material (a quaint term in vulgar use, meaning more or stronger men) then he should win. In theory, anyway.

This seems a good opportunity to examine a bona fide opening, at least for the first few moves, in which White goes for development at all costs.

	WHITE	BLACK
1.	**e4**	**e5**
2.	**d4**	**exd4**

The best move. Let us pause briefly to look at alternatives. Black might have tried to maintain a pawn on e5 by replying 2 . . . d6; when after 3. dxe5 dxe5; White could stop Black castling by exchanging queens.

If Black had played 2 . . . f6 with the same idea, he would have been justly punished. White would have continued 3. dxe5, fxe5 (better for Black not to recapture); 4. Qh5+. This early sortie with the queen is condoned for the reason given previously; there are defects in the opponent's position that can be immediately exploited. As we remarked earlier, the move f3/f6 is almost invariably bad. (You do know Fool's Mate, don't you? The shortest possible game of chess that no-one ever actually plays: 1. f3, e5; 2. g4, Qh4 mate.)

Now what is Black to do? If he blocks the queen with 4 . . . g6, White continues 5. Qxe5+ attacking both the king and the unguarded rook *(46)*.

On the other hand, if he moves the king to avoid the loss of the rook, the sequel is rather worse: 4 . . . Ke7; 5. Qxe5+, Kf7; 6. Bc4+, d5; (if the king moves to g6, White gives checkmate with the queen); 7. Bxd5+ and Black will still be mated in a few moves unless he gives up his queen *(47)*. A dreadful warning!

Another possibility might have been 2 . . . Nc6, when 3. d5 would have forced the knight to move again.

BLACK

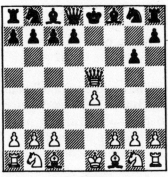

WHITE

46

BLACK

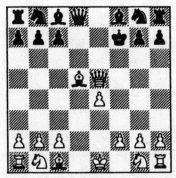

WHITE

47

Now return to the main line.

3.   c3

Instead of recapturing with the queen, when Black would gain time by attacking it with 3 . . . Nc6, White offers another pawn.

3.   . . .   dxc3

Black can here safely decline the gambit by, for example, striking in the centre with 3 . . . d5.

4.   Bc4

Yet another pawn on offer . . .

4.   . . .   cxb2

5.   Bxb2 *(48)*

Which side would you like to play? White has two finely posted bishops and is well ahead in development, but Black is two pawns to the good with no obvious weaknesses. However, he will have to play carefully or White's cavalier attack will bring home the bacon (the opening is called the Danish Gambit, by the way).

BLACK

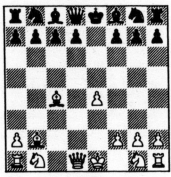

WHITE

48

Now turn the board round and look at the game from Black's side.

Black has a splendid move here which you probably would not have considered.

5.   ...   **d5!** *(49)*

What is the meaning of this? Black has a tactical resource which gives him at least equality but that apart, the move has an inherent logic. It forces an immediate response from White (otherwise the bishop is taken), threatens to exchange material (when you are ahead in material, exchanges are usually in your favour), and incidentally releases the QB. It is an axiom that the best way to meet and defeat a gambit is to give the material back at the right moment.

WHITE

BLACK

49

A plausible alternative for Black would have been 5 . . . Nf6, but then White had 6. e5, and Black is in trouble. Passive play will not do for either side in this situation. You can work out good replies for White in reply to 6 . . . d5, or 6 . . . Bb4+.

Back to the opening proper.

White has only one good alternative: to take the pawn with the bishop. To take it with the queen would invite an exchange of queens, drawing the sting from the attack, while to take it with the pawn would block the bishop, allowing Black to continue safely with Nf6.

6.   Bxd5   Nf6!

Black brings out the knight anyway! The position is highly tactical. Black wants to remove the dangerous white-squared bishop. If the bishop retreats, Black will exchange queens and then help himself to the king's pawn. White can remove the troublesome knight with his queen's bishop but Black will then recapture with the queen, attacking White's rook, gaining time to consolidate his position. Observe that 6 . . . Be6, would have been bad since it allows 7. Bxb7 and the black rook cannot escape. Similarly, 6 . . . Bd6, permits 7. Bxg7 with the same result! But White has a trick up his sleeve . . .

7.   Bxf7+   Kxf7

If the king had gone to e7 to keep guard on the queen but blocking his own bishop, White would have quickly gained the upper hand with 8. Qb3 (threatening 9. Ba3+, winning).

8.   Qxd8

Has White won the queen? Not quite . . .

8.   . . .   Bb4+ *(50)*

A discovered attack on the queen! So as not to lose a piece for nothing, White must retreat the queen . . .

WHITE

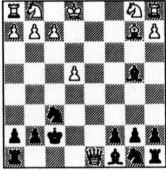

BLACK

50

9.	Qd2	Bxd2+
10.	Nxd2	

Here we will take our leave of the Danish. White has recovered his two pawns but Black has the better game since his extra pawns on the queen's side are more menacing than White's on the king's side. White has failed in his efforts to maintain the initiative conferred on him by the opening move thanks to Black's resourceful play. A model of how to gain time and how to get it back again.

FORKS AND THINGS

The openings are studded with tactical traps and man-oeuvres. Many of these are associated with specific lines of play but others recur time and again in a variety of situations and it is well to recognize them.

The fork, in which one man attacks two others simul-taneously, is a common tactical theme. An example of a pawn fork was demonstrated in *(35)* (page 20). A similar manoeuvre involves the temporary sacrifice of a piece in order to break open the centre. Here it is in simple form:

	WHITE	BLACK
1.	e4	e5
2.	Nc3	Nf6
3.	Bc4	Nxe4
4.	Nxe4	d5 *(51)*

However White plays, Black will recover the piece with a good position.

White need not have taken the knight immediately. He could have counter-sacrificed, for example, with 4. Bxf7+, Kxf7; 5. Nxe4, but then after 5 . . . d5 Black has a free game and a strong centre at the expense of a little temporary discomfort for his king.

This pawn fork can often lead to violent play, whether or not the sacrifice is accepted immediately. White's opening

WHITE

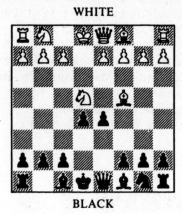

BLACK

51

here is called the Vienna and the usual line for the first player is to ignore the sacrifice on the theory that Black has lost time as he has moved the same piece twice in the first three moves.

Re-start with the first three moves above.

4.   Qh5

Having advised you against bringing your queen out early, here is another exception. Black's only good defence is to retreat the knight. This leaves it awkwardly placed – what is usually wrong about the move Qh5 is that sooner or later the opposing king's knight will appear on f6, attacking the queen and so gaining time.

4.   . . .   Nd6

Mate was threatened.

5.   Bb3

White can instead take the king's pawn with check, but after the reply Qe7, the queens must be exchanged and Black has no problems.

5.   . . .   Nc6
6.   d4   exd4

White presses his attack with a second pawn sacrifice. Black would have done better to take it with the knight, keeping the e-file closed to the attacker.

  7. Nd5   **g6**

An instructive blunder. The king is now fatally exposed due to the weakness of the black squares round about him.

  8. Qe2+   **Be7**

  9. Nf6+   **Kf8**

 10. Bh6 mate *(52)*

BLACK

WHITE

52

In the above example, the defence went down as the result of two poor moves. Just to redress the balance and to illustrate the tactical opportunities in this opening, the next line favours Black. First five moves as above. (1. e4, e5; 2. Nc3, Nf6; 3. Bc4, Nxe4; 4. Qh5, Nd6; 5. Bb3, Nc6).

  6. Nb5   **g6**

Now this move is forced but White has no damaging check.

7.   Qf3   **f5**

The black king position is exposed but White's queen is getting pushed around.

8.   Qd5   **Qe7**

White was threatening Nxd6+, and after the recapture to give mate with the queen at f7. Black's move guards against this but allows White to fork king and rook.

9.   Nxc7+   **Kd8**

10.   Nxa8   **b6** *(53)*

An extraordinary situation. Black is a rook in arrears though he will win the knight in exchange for a pawn. But wonder at his position! The two bishops can be developed speedily and the rook will come to the centre. White's queen will be in danger and he will have to move it again; meanwhile four of his pieces are still on their starting squares. The fact that Black cannot castle is irrelevant here. It is situations like this that illuminate the fascination of chess.

WHITE

BLACK

53

It is the privilege of chess writers, sometimes abused, to argue any theories they please and then prove them with carefully chosen samples of play. Here and always you should query and check every recorded move. Distrust is a better guide than faith. Often only one line of play will be analysed when there are clearly possible alternatives. Examine these alternatives (if you can't see any, look for them) and, if you have the opportunity, put into practice any that you think are sound. Query not just the moves but the sequence in which they are played. Even 'obvious' moves – like recapturing a queen – can sometimes be delayed with advantage; for example, by first intervening a check. The time to start thinking is at move one and the time to stop only when the game is over.

We saw another type of fork in *(46)* (page 31) where a queen simultaneously attacked king and rook. This kind of stratagem is dangerous because it can occur in a variety of guises and often at long range. Here is a dramatic example.

	WHITE	BLACK
1.	e4	c5
2.	d4	cxd4
3.	Nf3	

White does not want to recapture the pawn at once since Black will then gain time by developing his queen's knight.

3.	. . .	e5
4.	Nxe5	Qa5+ *(54)*

Winning the knight. Memo to yourself: monitor unguarded men and keep your attention travelling.

Undefended men are always a problem. There is a little ploy that over the years must have won millions of pawns and continues to find victims, even amongst experienced players, because it is unobvious. You know it, yet you overlook it. Here it is.

	WHITE	BLACK
1.	e4	e6
2.	d4	d5
3.	e5	c5
4.	c3	Nc6

Logical play. White has a good pawn structure with the apex towards the centre. Black, who has adopted the French

BLACK

WHITE

54

Defence, has succeeded in blocking the position and is now attempting to undermine the advanced pawn. In several openings, it is the deliberate strategy of the defence, as here, to permit the opponent to form an apparently strong pawn centre with the express intention of weakening, and eventually destroying it.

5.   Bb5   Bd7

Now the knight is free to move.

6.   Nf3

Natural – and calamitous.

6.   . . .   Nxe5 *(55)*

Winning the advanced pawn. If White captures the knight, he loses his bishop, and if he plays 7. Bxd7+, Black recaptures with the knight.

Watch for pieces that are overburdened – taking on more defence duties than they can manage. Positions similar to that in *(56)* occur quite often.

Black is underdeveloped, has a misplaced knight and is in considerable danger. If White were to play, he has the crushing 1. e5. The attacked knight cannot move without

BLACK

WHITE

55

WHITE

BLACK

56

loss of the queen. In like situations, Black can often get out of trouble by attacking the bishop: 1 . . . h6, and if 2. Bh4,

g5. If White now saves his bishop, Black rescues his knight.
Note this sequence carefully: many beginners abandon the
knight as doomed.

Here, alas, it does not work for Black, all because of that
misplaced knight. After 1 . . .h6 there follows 2. exf6, hxg5;
3. fxg7 *(57)* when Black's wretched KB has to look two ways
– at the pawn fork and at the knight it is defending. White
must win a piece in exchange for a pawn.

WHITE

BLACK

57

Suppose however it was Black's turn in *(56)*. Can you see
a weakness in the White position? The queen is simultaneously guarding the d-pawn and a threatened knight
fork. So Black can play Qxd4! His troubles are over, and
White's begin. If White captures Qxd4, Black now has the
fork Nc2+! followed, when the king moves, by Nxd4. It is
worth repeating that it often occurs that pieces are
overburdened in the openings.

Are you committing these positions to memory? I hope
not – it is only the ideas you are meant to be absorbing.

A MODEL OPENING

It is time to look at a model opening, an opening in which sound play on both sides leads to an approximately even position.

Why do players not always follow model openings? Because, as you may have noticed, people play chess and books don't. People have strengths and weaknesses, likes and dislikes, as well as indifferent memories. Are you aggressive? placid? adventurous? cautious? devious? impatient? ruthless? – then there is an opening or two that will suit your inclinations (they are called your 'style' when you play a bit better). But remember; at present you are engaged on an ecumenical exercise: you are experimenting with *all* openings so as to improve your standard of play rapidly.

The Ruy Lopez is five hundred years old and is claimed to be the opening in which White can maintain his initiative the longest. It is identified by these moves:

WHITE	BLACK
1. e4	e5
2. Nf3	Nc6
3. Bb5 *(58)*	

BLACK

WHITE

58

If White, instead of playing the bishop to b5, had played it one square short to c4, the play would have been transformed – one little square makes another world in the chess openings.

3.   . . .   a6

This humble move, the most favoured response for Black, seems to contradict our opening principles for it does not assist in the development of a piece nor does it strike at the centre. At a favourable moment, White might exchange the bishop for the knight and then capture the pawn on e5, though this will not work at once (4. Bxc6, dxc6; 5. Nxe5, Qd4) when Black regains the pawn with an excellent game *(59)*

WHITE

BLACK

59

Also, Black will soon want to move his d-pawn when the knight will be pinned against the king and could cause embarrassment. So 3 . . . a6 forces White to make up his mind at once.

Supposing he exchanges and then castles.

(A bishop and knight are approximately equal in value, so the term 'exchange' can fairly be used.)

4. Bxc6   **dxc6**

This move opens lines for the bishop and queen. To capture with the b-pawn would clear a file for the rook but would leave the a-pawn isolated. The text is better. (Notice that the centre pawn could still be recovered after 4 . . . bxc6; 5. Nxe5, Qe7, and if White defends the knight Black can attack it with a pawn.)

5. 0–0

Now what is a good move for Black? This time, White is threatening to take the pawn. Black's queen sortie (59) will no longer work since the knight can retreat to f3 and the e-pawn cannot be taken because White would answer Re1, winning queen for rook. Black has three possible replies in this position; Bg4, pinning the aggressive knight; Bd6, defending the pawn but placing the bishop passively; and, probably best, f6.

What, you say, f6? But haven't I been warned never to play that? Not quite: you must always consider the position on the board. There is nothing sacrosanct in the chess openings, which is why you need to question every move. Dogma is for dunderheads. The position, in the last analysis, is everything. (You are ahead in both development and material, you have a fine centre, lots of space in which to manoeuvre, and an irresistible attack – oh, bad luck, it's checkmate.)

Now for a different line from Black's third move. Play the first three moves again:

1. e4   **e5**
2. Nf3   **Nc6**
3. Bb5   **a6**

White could decline the exchange by retreating the bishop.

4. Ba4

Amongst experts, bishops are slightly preferred to knights, and two bishops much preferred to two knights, all other things equal. What has Black achieved by his third move? Something useful: he now has the option of playing b5 at any time to avoid the exchange should it be in his best interests to do so.

4.   . . .   Nf6
5.   0–0

White temporarily surrenders a pawn which Black can now take (5 . . . Nxe4). This line leads to sharp play, and is followed further on page 48.

5.   . . .   Be7

Black elects for safe development. The choice between these alternatives is a matter of taste (other moves are also playable but there is no room to discuss them here) and highlights an option that is often available to both sides in the openings – that between safe and adventurous play.

6.   Re1   b5
7.   Bb3   d6
8.   c3

White has got his king to safety and now plans to advance in the centre. This move is to support a pawn at d4.

8.   . . .   0–0
9.   h3

This move serves a dual purpose; it prevents an awkward pin and provides an escape square for the king against possible mating threats on the back rank later on. (A castled king, anchored behind a row of unmoved pawns, is vulnerable to a rook or queen arriving behind the lines.) However, this move is not to be encouraged as a prophylactic unless there is something painful threatened – here, Bg4.

9.   . . .   Na5
10.   Bc2

Black wants to counter in the centre. His ninth move frees the c-pawn and also attacks the bishop which White will not willingly surrender as Black's white-squared bishop would then become powerful.

Black's 6th move is now explained. If he had waited until White had played c3, White could have retreated the bishop at once to c2, thereby saving a move. White has now made four moves with his bishop while his queen's side pieces are yet undisturbed. However, his play earns no censure since

Black has made two pawn moves in pursuit of the bishop that do not contribute to the centre struggle and has moved his queen's knight to the board edge. Another example of give something, take something. Both sides are jockeying for position. *(60)*

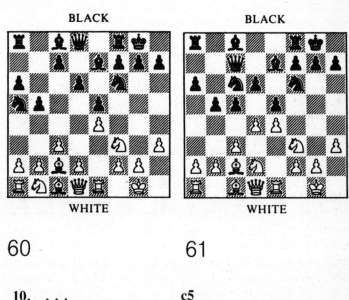

60   61

10.	...	c5
11.	d4	Qc7
12.	Nbd2	Nc6 *(61)*

Now White's d-pawn is under threat and he must decide whether to exchange it or to advance. This well-balanced position has been reached countless times in master play. Generally, White tries for an attack on the king's side, Black on the queen's, though it is what happens in the centre that will decide the course of the game. Notice that after twelve moves by both sides, all the men are still on the board and the pieces are grouped behind the pawns.

We noted that Black could have opted for sharp play at move 5. How would you, as White, have replied to this? Set the men back and start again.

	WHITE	BLACK
1.	e4	e5
2.	Nf3	Nc6
3.	Bb5	a6
4.	Ba4	Nf6
5.	0–0	Nxe4 (62)

BLACK　　　　　　　　WHITE

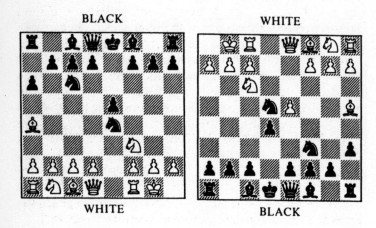

WHITE　　　　　　　　BLACK

62　　　　　　　　　63

White can regain the pawn in several ways, for example by moving the queen or rook to the e-file, but Black then gets easy equality, usually by retreating the king's knight to c5 where it attacks the white bishop. The best move here does not recover the pawn at once but instead hits immediately at the centre while Black is still uncastled.

6.　d4 (63)

How does the position now look from Black's side? Black would like to counter with 6 . . . d5 here, but this would open the position with his king still insecure. Now is the time to take advantage of his third move by freeing the knight.

| 6. | . . . | b5 |
| 7. | Bb3 | d5 |

8.   dxe5

White has got his pawn back.

8.   ...   Be6 *(65)*

The d-pawn is attacked twice. Not a good idea would be
8. . . . Ne7, preparing c6 to anchor the weak pawn. There
are two reasons: firstly, the move does not develop a piece
(the text does) and secondly, it blocks development of the
king's bishop, further delaying castling. (Black cannot
seriously consider castling on the queen's side because of
his pawn moves there; – kings suffer from agoraphobia.)

In these and similar circumstances, do not spend time
looking for tactical refutations on the argument that if you
cannot find any, the move is justified. If you must play
awkward moves that go against good sense, the best you can
hope for is a difficult game. Here it could be worse. For
example, 8. . . . Ne7?; 9. Re1, c6?; 10. Rxe4! and if 10. . . .
dxe4; 11. Bxf7+ *(64)* followed by Qxd8. If you make bad
positional moves, do not be surprised to find something
nasty lurking round the corner. (You would not have been
forgiven if you considered 8 . . . Nb4 as a way to guard the
d-pawn, 9. c3 would cost a piece as you may discover.)

After 8 . . . Be6 *(65)*; White has a choice of plans. One

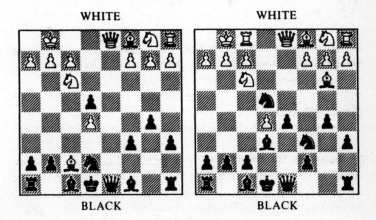

WHITE   WHITE

BLACK   BLACK

64   65

that may not occur to you is to move the queen to e2 and bring the rook to d1 to put pressure on Black's central pawn. However White plays, Black must hasten out his King's bishop, either to e7 or to c5.

A CLASSICAL GAMBIT

The King's Gambit is characterised by the moves

WHITE	BLACK
1. **e4**	**e5**
2. **f4**	

It was probably the most popular opening of the last century, when spirited play was expected of ladies and gentlemen who played chess. Many enterprising, even reckless, attacks and counter-attacks are associated with this gambit. Alas, most of these have now been refuted and the opening has lost popularity. From the novice's viewpoint, however, it is one of the best exercise yards on account of the sharpness of its play and the richness of its tactical ideas.

We have seen *(44)* (page 27) that White's second move is a little loosening, but in the King's Gambit everything is sacrificed on the altar of development, the first player striving for an early attack against Black's King, and Black frequently countering against White's king. On the queen's side, all is composure. After:

2. ...	**exf4**
3. **Nf3**	

the basic position in the gambit accepted is reached. *(66)*

Black can now try to hang on to his extra pawn, which is something of a wedge in the white position, by the ugly yet effective

3. ...	**g5**

The trouble with this move is – what? Of course: it does not develop a piece nor does it contest the centre (it seems one must have a lot of exceptions to prove the rule).

BLACK

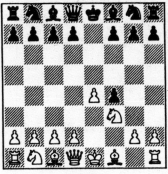

WHITE

66

The move belongs to the trumpet days of the gambit. It is understandably frowned on by today's purists.

4. Bc4   g4

Against all principles, of course, but still playable. Now 5. Ne5 is not advisable because of 5 . . . Qh4+; 6. Kf1 Nh6; and Black is doing very nicely. Notice that although this knight has been developed to the side of the board, it defends two threatened pawns. White can now hardly be enjoying the prospect of 7 . . . d6. Here is the sort of tactical variation that could follow: 7. d4, Bg7; 8. Bxf4, d6; 9. Bxh6, Bxh6; 10. Nxf7, Rf8 and the knight is pinned. Best play? Of course not, but plausible. Note carefully that White could not play 10. Bxf7+ because after 10 . . . Kf8 or 10 . . . Ke7, the bishop or knight is lost.

5. 0–0!   gxf3

6. Qxf3 (67)

White is a piece down but far ahead in development. This sparkling gambit (thanks to our imaginative ancestors many gambits that are offshoots of the King's Gambit have been granted recognition) is known as the Muzio. In practice, it is hard to defend against. Isn't chess difficult?

BLACK

WHITE

67

Return to the basic gambit position *(66)*.

White's third move prevents a discomforting check from the black queen, so another idea for Black:

3.   ...   **Be7**

Without the gambit pawn, the threatened check would be worthless because of the reply g3. Now the check cannot be stopped except by h4 or g3, either of which would severely weaken White's king's side where he is committed to castle. So White allows the check – and offers two further pawns in the process!

4.   **Bc4**   **Bh4+**
5.   **g3**   **fxg3**
6.   **0–0**   **gxh2+**
7.   **Kh1** *(68)*

The king finds sanctuary behind the pawn; to capture it with either king or knight would be indecent since it would leave the king naked. Black would now be wise to start shedding pawns to speed his own development before it is too late. On this logic, 7 . . . d5 is the right move here.

Notice that the black bishop is something of a liability. It

BLACK

WHITE

68

is not doing much now and it must be kept guarded as it is under attack from the knight, or lose more time by retreating. It would have been a mistake for White to have taken the bishop 5. Nxh4 on account of 5. . . . Qxh4+; and White must forgo castling since 6. g3, fxg3; 7. 0–0, Qxh2 is mate.

An adequate defensive system for Black is to take the pawn and then counter at once in the centre. From *(66)* we get

3.	. . .	d5
4.	exd5	

And now either 4 . . . Nf6 or 4 . . . Bd6 is constructive, the one attacking the centre, the other reinforcing the advanced pawn, and both developing a piece.

White can stop both these moves by simply advancing his e-pawn instead of capturing but Black would then wisely revert to 4 . . . g5 *(69)*, the difference now being that he has a share of the centre and his d-pawn stops White's bishop occupying its best square (c4) from where it would menace the Black king position. The conclusion is that 4. e5 is not a good idea for White. Black stands very well.

WHITE   WHITE

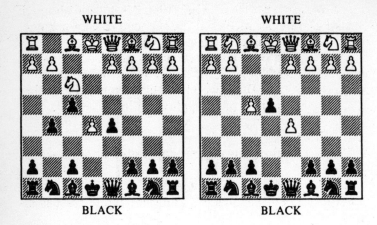

BLACK   BLACK

69   70

The gambit can be equally well declined. A popular way of doing this is for Black to play 2. . . . d5 (we are back to the pawn structure of *44*) (page 27). This is known as the Falkbeer and is really a counter-gambit.

3.   exd5   e4 *(70)*

This move prevents the natural development of the king's knight. White's f-pawn does not look so threatening now. The reply 3. fxe5 would have been answered fearsomely with Qh4+ followed by Qxe4.

4.   d3   Nf6
5.   dxe4   Nxe4
6.   Be3

The alternative is the natural 6. Nf3 but this leaves the black diagonal looking dangerous after 6 . . . Bc5. Now Black has a tactical variation to equalize.

6.   . . .   Qh4+
7.   g3

White must not move the king or he walks into a knight fork. 7. Ke2?, Ng3+; 8. hxg3, Qxh1. If White then tries to harass the queen by 9. Nh3, her counterpart is skewered with 9 . . . Bg4+. The more promising 9. Kf2 permits the

queen to escape with 9 . . . Qh6; 10. f5?, Qf6; and although
Black has only his queen out, he is ahead (rook for knight
and pawn) and White's king's side pawns are in ruins.

Another idea; instead of 9 . . . Qh6, Black could try the
immediate attack 9 . . . h5, but now White has 10. Nf3 and
if 10 . . . Bg4, it is Black who loses his queen to 11. Bb5+.

Returning to the main line, play continues

   7.   . . .   **Nxg3**

   8.   Nf3

This is a useful tactical trick, not confined to the King's
Gambit.

   8.   . . .   **Qe7**

If Black keeps his queen on the file, White rescues his
rook.

   9.   hxg3   **Qxe3+**

  10.   Qe2 *(71)*

and the queens get exchanged to yield an even game. Never
be reluctant to exchange queens if the situation demands it.
10. Be2?; Bc5 and White is in a tangle.

BLACK

WHITE

71

Another good way to decline the gambit is by 2. . . . Bc5, for White cannot take the pawn at once on account of Qh4+. If you move your f-pawn before you castle, be on the lookout for this check.

TYPES OF POSITION

It would be convenient if one could stereotype opening positions and then draw up, as it were, codes of behaviour for each type of position. This cannot be done, but openings are sometimes described as 'open' or 'close' and here it is possible to establish a few guidelines.

Open and close are rather vague terms. An open game is generally taken to mean a game in which the minor pieces (knights and bishops) are developed in front of the pawns and there is an early exchange of at least one pair of pawns to create an open file which rooks can look down.

A close game is one in which the minor pieces are mostly grouped behind the pawns which may also be locked in a rigid pawn skeleton.

Look back at the Ruy Lopez previously described. The first few moves confirm this as an open game. In one of the main lines however *(61)* (page 47) we reached a position where the pieces had retreated behind their pawn screens. So what type of game is it? Answer – an open game with a closed defence. Call it ajar. Many openings mix the characteristics of the two; they are part open, part close. It doesn't of course matter what you call any of them but it is useful to appreciate the different strategies demanded.

In open games, speedy development of the pieces is usually paramount. Space is important too. A cramped position reduces mobility and can lead to strangulation.

In close games, the central pawns are usually locked together and there is a lack of open lines on which the rooks and bishops can operate effectively. Attacks cannot be quickly assembled which means that the importance of the time factor is reduced. Instead of striving for quick development, which may not be possible anyway, the aim in close games is often to get the pieces on the right squares even if in some cases this may take several moves.

Space is also less of a problem but the pawn structure is, if anything, more important than in open games. Sooner or later it is likely that one side will unzip the position, perhaps with a sacrifice, when the speed with which key pieces can penetrate behind the lines may well decide the game. An example of a close game may help to make things clearer.

A CLOSE GAME

	WHITE	BLACK
1.	d4	d5
2.	e3	

This rather passive move at once declares White's intentions. He plans to lock the centre and develop an attack on the king's side. A disadvantage of this plan is that Black will have little difficulty in achieving equality.

	WHITE	BLACK
2.	. . .	Nf6
3.	Bd3	c5

It is right for Black to react vigorously in situations like this. Also, it is often a good idea (for both sides) to move the c-pawn forward before bringing out the queen's knight, though on this occasion White has other ideas.

	WHITE	BLACK
4.	c3	Nc6
5.	f4	

This system, known as the Stonewall (you can play it also as Black), seeks an early control of e5 to prevent the defence freeing the centre by advancing e5.

	WHITE	BLACK
5.	. . .	e6

This move shuts in the queen's bishop. But, you say, surely White's queen's bishop is also incarcerated? So what's the difference? The difference is that it is White's king's bishop that is dangerous and should be countered. 5 . . . Bg4 is much better. After White develops the knight, Black will play e6 and then retreat his bishop to f5 to face his white rival.

6.	Nf3	Bd6
7.	Nbd2	0–0
8.	Ne5	Bd7 (72)

BLACK

WHITE

72

The game is closed at present, and a problem with all such positions is to find a satisfactory way to make progress. A little thought will show that Black, who has developed rather mechanically, can only do this by first retreating the knight to e8 and then advancing the f-pawn. The knight at f6 is a stout defender of a castled king and in particular guards the weak pawn at h7, so a retreat with this knight will temporarily weaken the king's side: timing will therefore be critical.

White on the other hand faces no threats to his king and can set about preparing an attack, perhaps with g4. White would not want to exchange off his well-posted knight for the impotent queen's bishop.

The main problem on White's side is getting the queen's bishop and rook into play. In closed positions, these pieces are often confined to home for much of the game.

A PSEUDO GAMBIT

The King's Gambit, as we saw, is not without its attendant risks for White. On the other side of the board, the Queen's Gambit is a relatively tame affair. Like in the King's Gambit, White's second move strikes immediately at the Black centre; here however the move carries few hazards for the first player but equally rewards can be harder earned.

The first point to note about the Queen's Gambit is that it is hardly a gambit at all since the second player would be unwise to attempt to hold the pawn for long. The opening moves are:

	WHITE	BLACK
1.	d4	d5
2.	c4	dxc4

The gambit can be safely accepted, but let's see what happens if Black tries to cling to the pawn.

3.	e3	b5

Compare the King's Gambit. One difference is that the pawn advance in no way threatens White's king. White must strike at once before Black can consolidate.

4.	a4	c6
5.	axb5	cxb5
6.	Qf3 *(73)*	

– and Black must give up a piece. Notice that 4 . . . a6 would have been answered by 5. axb5 when Black could not recapture without losing his rook.

Did you wonder about the possibility of playing 4 . . .

BLACK

WHITE

73

bxa4? Start again and then make the capture 4 . . . bxa4 instead of 4 . . . c6. Now look at the resultant pawn skeleton. It's more like a collection of old bones, isn't it?

None of Black's queen's side pawns protects, or can move to protect, any other. They could hardly be worse placed. (Pawns are strongest abreast or in a diagonal line with their apex towards the centre.) White can regain the two pawns he has sacrificed with ease and will also get much the better position. For example, after 4. . . . bxa4? 5. Bxc4, Black's advanced rook's pawn is 'en prise' (chess shorthand for saying it is unguarded and can be taken for nothing). If Black tries to save it with 5. . . . Bd7, White moves 6. Qf3, simultaneously threatening checkmate at f7 (that weak point again!) and attacking the undefended rook. An attempt to parry both threats with 6. . . . Bc6; fails against 7. Qxf7+, Kd7 *(74)* and you can have the pleasure of discovering how White can now force mate in two more moves.

If you have been colour-conscious, you may have observed a feature of these variations. All Black's weaknesses were on white squares, a direct consequence of his

BLACK

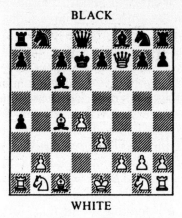

WHITE

74

third move b5. Was there not, you may ask, a corresponding weakening of the black squares in the King's Gambit where Black played g5 *(66)* (page 51)? The answer is a cautious 'yes', but with an important distinction. White was committed there to castling on the king's side whereas here he would be foolish even to consider castling on the queen's side. Why not? Because the position is too open and two pawns, valuable as shields for a castled king, have departed.

A weakness is only a weakness if the other side can take advantage of it. Weaknesses can be temporary or permanent. Because pawns cannot retreat, and as often as not cannot advance without loss, pawn weaknesses are more likely to be permanent than piece weaknesses – that is, pieces posted on bad squares. Once a pawn has surrendered guard on a square it can never regain it.

So although the variations we have just been looking at were tactical, their origins were positional. From this we can draw a useful conclusion: positional weaknesses create tactical opportunities. From here we can proceed to the idea of provoking positional weaknesses as a viable strategy.

Try to force or entice disabling pawn advances and get the opponents' pieces onto bad squares – the tactical combinations that win material or perhaps lead to mate, will then present themselves. Masters play positional chess as a matter of course – they would never achieve mastery unless they did. In your games, you are in the habit, from time to time, of overlooking lethal checks and undefended men, and probably hope that your opponent will do likewise which is why you are inclined to play on long after you should have given up. Strong players rarely overlook such things. When they crack it is usually because their position has become untenable, like Black's in the opening we have been looking at.

While you are thinking about that, follow through the next opening which is something a little more orthodox. Again a Queen's Gambit, but this time Black declines the pawn and instead fortifies the centre.

	WHITE	BLACK
1.	d4	d5
2.	c4	e6

If Black had defended with 2 . . . Nf6, White would have captured in the centre and then brought out the queen's knight or advanced the king's pawn, depending on whether Black recaptured with the queen or knight respectively, so gaining time.

	WHITE	BLACK
3.	Nc3	Nf6
4.	Bg5	Nbd7

Doesn't that lose a pawn?

	WHITE	BLACK
5.	cxd5	exd5
6.	Nxd5	Nxd5!
7.	Bxd8	Bb4+
8.	Qd2	Bxd2+
9.	Kxd2	Kxd8 (75)

White has lost a piece for a pawn. Black could have played instead 8. . . . Kxd8 since the white queen cannot escape. Sometimes it is wise to defer a capture under these circumstances.

Do not seek any profound meaning in this little trap, but it

BLACK

WHITE

75

serves to remind you that there can be pitfalls in the most innocent-looking positions. Never play 'obvious' moves without taking a second look.

A more natural move for Black, since it prepares to castle and does not block a piece, is 4 . . . Be7. Let's start again.

WHITE	BLACK
1. d4	d5
2. c4	e6
3. Nc3	Nf6
4. Bg5	Be7

Exemplary play by both sides. White is putting pressure on Black's centre and is in no hurry to develop his king's side pieces since his king is not in danger. Black has a small problem – how to develop his queen's bishop effectively. A feature of the gambit accepted is that this bishop can be developed before moving the e-pawn, a benefit offset by ceding temporary advantage in the centre to White – the 'give and take' syndrome. Another idea: Black can defer the capture of the gambit pawn until after White has developed his king's bishop, forcing it to move again. White on the other hand will not be keen to anticipate this by playing cxd5 since this would allow Black to recapture with his e-pawn, so freeing the bishop.

Black plans to free his bishop by advancing the e-pawn at the right moment. He cannot do this while his d-pawn is under threat. You should now be able to follow the logic behind the next few moves.

5.	Nf3	0–0
6.	e3	Nbd7
7.	Rc1	c6
8.	Bd3	dxc4
9.	Bxc4	Nd5
10.	Bxe7	Qxe7
11.	0–0	Nxc3
12.	Rxc3	e5 *(76)*

WHITE

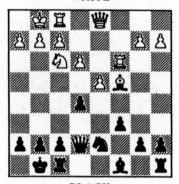

BLACK

76

Black has achieved his objective though White still has a faint edge. You should experiment with other ideas for Black; for example, by playing b6 and bringing the bishop into play via b7 – this placing of the bishop is known as the fianchetto. Also, did you wonder at the purpose of the passive 7 . . . c6? Without that white rook looking down the file you could have considered c5.

Whatever you do as Black, you must not allow your queen's bishop to be shut in (White has no such problems). A piece out of play is a piece minus. Even if you are ahead in material, do not be tempted into complacency. Untold games have been won by the side with the weaker forces. It is usually the case that the winner has been able to concentrate his forces in the right place at the right time. What's the good of being a rook and a bishop ahead if both are on their original squares when your king gets mated in the middle of the board?

AN ORTHODOX OPENING

The next opening, known as the Four Knights for obvious reasons, can be described as orthodox because it follows closely an opening axiom that has been around a long time: knights out first, then bishops. Like a lot of good advice it is hardly profound since this is the natural order of things anyway – the knights develop freely and the mandatory pawn advance in the centre will release at least one bishop. It is an axiom to honour in the spirit but, as we have seen, not always in the letter.

	WHITE	BLACK
1.	e4	e5
2.	Nf3	Nc6
3.	Nc3	Nf6
4.	Bb5	Bb4
5.	0–0	0–0
6.	d3	d6 *(77)*

Symmetrical play and model development. Does this suggest to you that a good strategy for Black might be to imitate White's moves? Forget it. It may indeed be wise on occasion to copy your opponent's play for a few moves but only if your moves can be justified in their own right. In any

BLACK

WHITE

77

case, the strategy will fail sooner or later if only because the first player gives check. As an example, 1. e4, e5; 2. d4, d5; 3. dxe5, dxe4; 4. Qxd8+. How is Black going to mimic that? Or again, 1. e4, e5; 2. d4, d5; 3. exd5, exd4; 3. Qxd4 and Black is hardly likely to be tempted by 4 . . . Qxd5.

Let us continue . . .

| 7. | Bg5 | Bg4 |
| 8. | Nd5 | |

Now White threatens to capture soon on f6 with one of his pieces, forcing Black to recapture with the pawn, thereby gravely weakening the black squares around the king and exposing him to attack up the file. Black must perforce continue to ape White's play.

8.	. . .	Nd4
9.	Nxb4	Nxb5
10.	Nd5	Nd4
11.	Qd2 (78)	

Dare Black continue 11 . . . Qd7? He dare not. 11 . . . Qd7; 12. Bxf6, Bxf3; 13. Ne7+ (now the dance must stop), Kh8; 14. Bxg7+, Kxg7; 15. Qg5+, Kh8; 16. Qf6 mate. A bit

BLACK

WHITE

78

drastic, but it proves the point. Don't take this as any sort of norm – ten successive imitative moves is rare indeed.

None of the rooks took any part in the play. This is not at all unusual in a short game. Tucked away in the wings when the curtain goes up, the rooks are usually the last actors to come on stage.

THE QUIET GAME

The favourite opening to initiate beginners is the Giuoco Piano, the 'Quiet Game', one of the first openings ever recorded. Its potentialities are near to exhaustion – at least, that is the present view – so it does not appear often in master practice. However, the opening is popular amongst less-exalted chessplayers and rightly so, since, apart from being sound, it adheres closely to all the principles of good

opening play. It is not always as quiet as its name suggests –
you can get some quite wild games with the Giuoco Piano.

	WHITE	BLACK
1.	e4	e5
2.	Nf3	Nc6
3.	Bc4	Bc5
4.	c3 *(79)*	

This is a lively continuation.

BLACK

WHITE

79

The text takes away the best square for the queen's knight
but the deprivation is temporary. White's aggressive
intentions are obvious, Black's defence less so. The dozy 4.
d3 would allow Black to develop undisturbed.

| 4. | . . . | Nf6 |

It is a good general rule that when you are perplexed for
a move, perhaps because the impending complications
extend out of sight, opt for the natural one – as here, it is
probably best.

| 5. | d4 | exd4 |
| 6. | cxd4 | |

You can see that to take with the knight would be out of
harmony with the idea behind White's fourth move. Also,

White has no intention of donating his e-pawn without a proper return.

6.	. . .	**Bb4+**
7.	**Nc3**	**Nxe4**
8.	**0–0**	**Bxc3**
9.	**d5** *(80)*	

White is a piece and a pawn behind – but not for long. The text keeps the attack going and has the virtue of denying Black the freeing d5. Not everyone's idea of a quiet game.

| 9. | . . . | **Bf6** |
| 10. | **Re1** | |

Keeping up the pressure. Black still has two pieces attacked.

| 10. | . . . | **Ne7** |

Black must be very careful for his king is still in the centre. An easy mistake here would be 10 . . . Ne5; 11. Nxe5, Bxe5; 12. Rxe4 with 13. f4 after Black defends the bishop.

| 11. | **Rxe4** | **d6** *(81)* |

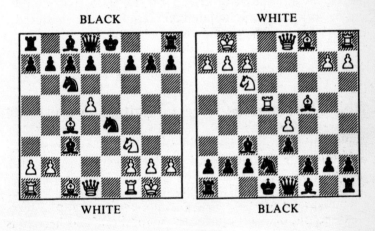

80   81

Let us assess the position. Black has scrambled a defence and is now prepared to castle. White has more space, a strong centre (although his king's bishop is temporarily blocked) and is well ahead in development – but he is a pawn short, which leaves the chances approximately even.

The problem for White is to find a weak point which his superior mobility will allow him to exploit. Time is at a premium. Black's pawn skeleton is uncompromised and his minor pieces will soon find good squares, and if that happens the extra pawn should begin to make its presence felt.

It is normal for a knight to be posted at f3/f6 rather than a bishop. There a knight defends the h-pawn, often the weak point in a castled position. (The weak point in the position of an uncastled king is f2/f7, the focus of many opening attacks.)

So White here has a target of sorts – the h-pawn. This leads sensibly to White's next move.

12.	Bg5	Bxg5
13.	Nxg5	

Black has been forced to exchange off his only developed piece. The alternative of 12 . . . 0–0; 13. Bxf6, gxf6, could not be seriously contemplated on account of the shattered pawn defences. The position is about level.

AN OUTRAGEOUS GAMBIT

An otherwise respectable sea captain, called Evans, is credited with the outrageous gambit which has borne his name for the last 150 years. The Evans is a bold alternative for White at the fourth move of the Giuoco Piano.

	WHITE	BLACK
1.	e4	e5
2.	Nf3	Nc6
3.	Bc4	Bc5
4.	b4 *(82)*	

This intemperate advance turns out to be not only playable but positively dangerous, requiring careful play by

Black. To decline the pawn is to give White a considerable advantage in space.

It is a general, though by no means universal principle that the best way to defuse a gambit is to accept it and then to return the material at a propitious moment.

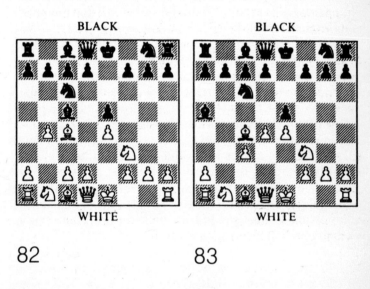

BLACK   BLACK

WHITE   WHITE

82   83

4. . . .   **Bxb4**

If 4 . . . Nxb4; White continues as in the main variation, with advantage. He must not be tempted by 5. Nxe5?, Qf6!; and now White cannot reply 6. d4 on account of 6 . . . Bxd4; 7. Qxd4, Nxc2+; followed by Nxd4 – that fork again! No better is 5. Nxe5?, Qf6!; 6. Bxf7+, Kf8; and Black has too many threats.

5. c3   **Ba5**

6. d4 *(83)*

The play hereon can get highly involved. White has sacrificed for rapid development and must turn this to advantage whereas Black will be anxious to get his king to safety as quickly as possible. In similar positions White can sometimes delay or even arrest Black castling by Ba3.

Always be on the look out for ideas like this and see if they can be made to work, it is not a bad way to tackle the openings. Contemplate ideal squares for your men then plan to get them there. If you can't, look round for a second-best plan.

For example, in *(83)* Black might reasonably decide that his priority is to castle. To do this he must bring the knight out. Is 6 . . . Nf6 playable? No, because after 7. dxe5, Nxe4; 8. Qd5 the stray knight is forfeit on account of the threat 9. Qxf7 mate. So the weakness on e5 must first be attended to. There appear to be two reasonable alternatives; 6 . . . exd4, removing the aggressor and also stopping White's queen reaching d5; and 6 . . . d6, which anchors the e-pawn. In fact, both these moves are playable.

It is a popular myth that chess masters examine in depth all the possible moves for both sides at each turn of play. Most possibilities the expert dismisses at a glance on the strength of his experience (which you are just starting to accumulate) or instinct (which is subconscious experience). Only when he has welded his ideas into a plan does he actually look at move sequences. You should try to do this too. Always have a plan. A bad plan is better than no plan at all, as every chess writer has counselled since the introduction of moveable type. Beware the King-Kong approach of 'Time-I-moved-the-bishop-where-shall-I-move-it-to?'

A TEMPTING TARGET

One plan that might occur to you is to attack f7, the weak point in the enemy defences, with minor pieces. (You scorn the idea of an immediate attack on it with the queen – a beginner's folly.)

	WHITE	BLACK
1.	e4	e5

2.	Nf3	Nc6
3.	Bc4	Nf6
4.	Ng5	

This move offends our opening precepts but f7 is a tempting target.

A threat can be met in one of two ways, and sometimes both simultaneously: it can be resisted or it can be ignored in favour of a counter attack. Surprisingly, Black has an adequate counter here in 4 . . . Bc5, striking at White's weak point. (If you want to know more, you will have to look up a heavy book on the openings!) But let's see what happens if Black resists.

4.	. . .	d5
5.	exd5	Nxd5

Black does better to attack the bishop with 5 . . . Na5 and complicated play to follow. Now White is faced with a further and bigger temptation.

6.	Nxf7	Kxf7
7.	Qf3+	Ke6

The knight is twice attacked and must be defended.

8.	Nc3	Nb4
9.	Qe4 *(84)*	

BLACK

WHITE

84

White guards against the knight fork of king and rook and prepares to drive the piece back with 10. a3. Moreover, White threatens d4 and then, if necessary, f4 or Bf4 when Black's pinned e-pawn will fall. Now Black has only 9 . . . c6 to save his piece and he must abide the coming storm. In practice, White is likely to win.

Something more must be said about White's fourth move. Apart from deflecting a piece from the centre and failing to implement development, this knight adventure fractures another opening maxim: 'do not move any piece twice until you've moved every piece once'. In few openings can this advice be followed literally, but the principle is a good one just the same.

In this case the move works because there is a clear reason behind it. To delay the attack would be to forgo it. We remarked earlier that it is sometimes wise to postpone a move, but the reverse is more often true. Be awake to opportunity; if your opponent lifts his guard you are likely to have only that one chance to take advantage of it. Developing your pieces is fine, but routine development is myopic. Remember to think through every move.

But to return to that knight move. As a general rule, the move Nb5/g5, or Nb4/g4 by Black, is a deplorable beginners' habit. Sometimes quite vacuous, sometimes aimed at a fork on c7/f7, or c2/f2 by Black, if the opponent obliges, the move is usually no more than a time-wasting gesture. The sortie can be justified only if it constitutes a threat. If the threat is easily countered, then a valid excuse for the move might be to advance the c/f-pawn with the intention of withdrawing the knight behind it.

STORM IN THE CENTRE

Another idea for White in this opening is to strike at once in the centre. This can lead to the Max Lange attack where things like positional play and pawn skeletons are temporarily abandoned in a lively punch-up.

	WHITE	BLACK
1.	e4	e5
2.	Nf3	Nc6
3.	Bc4	Nf6
4.	d4	exd4
5.	0–0	Bc5
6.	e5 *(85)*	

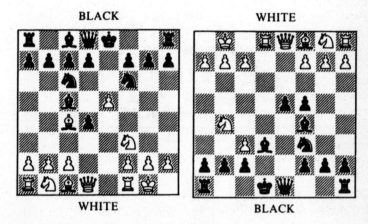

BLACK   WHITE

WHITE   BLACK

85   86

6. . . .   d5

The counter attack. Now things get a bit hairy.

7.	exf6	dxc4
8.	Re1+	Be6
9.	Ng5	

Another example of a justified knight advance. White can safely delay fxg7 – can't he?

9. . . .   Qd5

I hope you considered, and rejected, 9 . . . Qxf6?; 10. Nxe6, fxe6; 11. Qh5+ – see the undefended bishop?

10.   Nc3!

The knight cannot be taken because the pinned bishop does not defend the queen.

| **10.** | **. . .** | **Qf5** |
| **11.** | **Nce4** | **0–0–0** *(87)* |

WHITE

BLACK

87

A case where queen's side castling is called for. To castle on the king's side in face of White's wicked pawn would be suicidal. The pawn could still not be safely taken; 11. . . . gxf6?; 12. g4. Now the queen is overloaded and Black must lose a piece – or worse. Work out the alternatives.

ORDER, PLEASE!

The key position in the Max Lange *(85)* can be reached by playing the opening moves in any of several different orders. The sequence in which moves are made is nearly always important. Where this is not the case, you may still, by playing move A before B, either permit or deny options to your opponent.

It can happen that identical positions can be reached from quite different openings, perhaps with colours reversed, and not just different sequences of moves within the same opening. This is known in chess jargon as transposition. If you are playing the opening intelligently, as I trust you now are, a transposition should be of passing academic interest, but recognition that one has occurred may help you to focus onto the possibilities. To take a simple case, supposing you began 1. f4 (Bird's Opening, named after its practitioner, not because it's on the wing). Your opponent could reply with 1 . . . e5. This is an ingenious gambit. If you take the pawn at once (2. fxe5), Black continues with 2 . . . d6; when after 3. exd6, Bxd6, Black is threatening mate in three starting with a queen check and gets a good game for the pawn sacrificed. Perhaps that prospect does not appeal to you? Never mind: you have the possibility of transposing into the King's Gambit with 2. e4, which may not appeal to Black who perhaps for this reason deliberately avoids replying to 1. e4 with 1 . . . e5. This leads us on to consider psychology as a weapon in the chess openings.

KNOW YOUR ENEMY

In your choice of an opening or defence there are a number of extraneous factors to think about not least of which is your opponent, a rather complex organism who may at the same time be thinking about you.

Psychology can play a significant role in a chess game, and particularly in the opening. Masters sometimes ponder their first few moves (which are second nature to them) on this account.

On one occasion, a tournament game opened 1. e4, e6; 2. Bb5. The rationale behind White's extraordinary second move was that Black, a rigid theoretician, invariably responded 2 . . . d5 in this opening and could not now do so. More, if the bishop were driven away so that Black could proceed with his plan, it would inevitably move to a better square. The master who was playing Black was therefore faced with a dilemma. He spent 15 minutes over his reply and eventually lost.

This is not an example to emulate, merely an extreme case of psychology that paid off. If you have heeded the advice at the start of this book and are prepared to experiment with all openings you will be to some extent immune from shock tactics. If your opponent is a chess computer, then the risk of it exploiting your psychological weaknesses is minimal, though I wouldn't bank on that state of affairs lasting for ever. At this stage in your chess career it would be wiser to forget your opponent altogether and play the position before you. You are concerned with gaining experience, not with winning games – that will come later.

A PAWN CHARGE

A chess game is an indivisible conflict. For convenience, one talks of the opening, the middle game and the end game, but in practice the divisions are blurred and largely meaningless. In planning your first moves you should consider their long- as well as their short-term consequences. Pawn advances in particular require that you take a distant perspective.

The idea behind many opening variations is to establish an end-game advantage, and that is almost certain to include a superior pawn skeleton. A passed pawn – one that cannot be stopped in its march to promotion by an opposing pawn – is always strong provided it can be supported, for it needs a piece to check its progress, a distasteful duty for the defence.

Advanced pawns can be game winners – or losers. In the ending, when the queens have left the board and risk of checkmate is negligible, the kings become powerful pieces. Forward pawns whose support is weak or cut can be destroyed by an invading king when your king is likely to be far from the scene. It is important to consider the after-effects of what appears to be a promising advance.

Let us get one thing clear – and it deserves capitals – PASSIVE DEFENCE INVARIABLY FAILS. This applies to all openings and nowhere is it better illustrated than when facing a pawn charge. At times of course you are obliged to ward off threats with wretched little moves that create pawn weaknesses or involve humiliating retreats. But if you fix firmly the idea that a menacing pawn can, with vigorous counterplay, be turned into a distressed stray, then you are going to be looking for the right sort of moves.

	WHITE	BLACK
1.	d4	Nf6
2.	c4	g6
3.	Nc3	Bg7
4.	e4	d6
5.	f4 *(88)*	

WHITE

BLACK

88

Frightening, isn't it? Keep cool. Here you might consider
5. . . . c5, hitting at once at White's active centre but let's
suppose that you decide to remove your king from the path
of the avalanche. This formation for Black is quite common
against openings which begin with 1. d4. It offers security
and prepares to contest the centre with either e5 or c5. To
omit both would invite suffocation.

5.	. . .	0–0
6.	Nf3	c6
7.	Be2	Nfd7
8.	Be3	e5
9.	fxe5	dxe5
10.	d5	f5
11.	Qb3	Na6
12.	0–0–0 *(89)*	

BLACK   WHITE

WHITE   BLACK

89   90

Black's counter in the centre was tardy. Now White has
the certain prospect of a dangerous passed pawn on the
d-file.

On the other hand, an early advance by White, pushing
Black back, could prove premature for the cramp may only
be temporary. Continue from *(88)*.

5.	. . .	0–0
6.	e5	Ne8
7.	Be3	c5

This pawn sacrifice crumbles White's centre and is justified because White is behind in development – all his king's side pieces are still indoors.

8. dxc5

Black cannot recapture because his queen is unguarded – so he develops another piece.

8.	. . .	Nc6
9.	cxd6	exd6 *(90)*

Play might continue 10. Nf3, Qa5; 11. exd6, Nxd6; 12. Qxd6, Bxc3+; 13. bxc3, Qxc3+ followed by Qxa1. This fork of king and rook is a recurring theme in the openings. Observe that after 10. Nf3, dxe5? would not be a good idea. 11. Qxd8, Nxd8; and White has 12. Bc5, winning rook for bishop, yet another common theme in the openings. On the field of strategy, the ground is thick with tactics.

It is a widely held belief that the first several moves of a chess game are dull. After all, each side is just concerned with getting its pieces out; the fun starts later. The idea of pawn promotion, for example, seems absurd. How can a humble foot soldier advancing but one step at a time hope, in the early stages of a game, to break through the massed ranks of the enemy and achieve glory? To show you what can happen, given a lot of imagination and a little luck, here are two enthronements, the same theme in different openings and on opposite sides of the board.

	WHITE	BLACK
1.	d4	d5
2.	Nf3	Bf5
3.	c4	c6
4.	Qb3	Qb6
5.	cxd5	Qxb3
6.	axb3	Bxb1
7.	dxc6	Be4
8.	Rxa7!	Rxa7
9.	c7 and queens *(91)*	

BLACK   **WHITE**

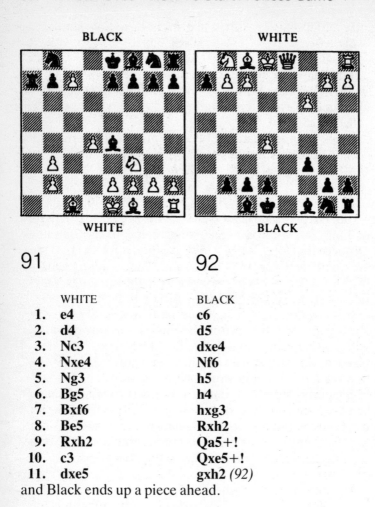

WHITE   BLACK

91   92

	WHITE	BLACK
1.	e4	c6
2.	d4	d5
3.	Nc3	dxe4
4.	Nxe4	Nf6
5.	Ng3	h5
6.	Bg5	h4
7.	Bxf6	hxg3
8.	Be5	Rxh2
9.	Rxh2	Qa5+!
10.	c3	Qxe5+!
11.	dxe5	gxh2 (92)

and Black ends up a piece ahead.

A COMBATIVE DEFENCE

The Sicilian Defence is characterised by 1. . . . c5, in answer
to 1. e4 (14) (page 11). It is a popular Black reply to White's
opening move. It creates an immediate imbalance in the

centre and usually leads to a lively if not exciting game.

WHITE	BLACK
1. **e4**	**c5**
2. **Nf3**	**Nc6**
3. **d4** *(93)*	

WHITE

BLACK

93

Not good would have been 2. d4, cxd4; 3. Qxd4, Nc6; when the queen must move again – but you knew that, didn't you? White could have instead prepared d4 with 2. c3 but that would have allowed Black to continue 2 . . . d5; and after 3. exd5, Qxd5; White is deprived of the time-gaining Nc3.

To establish pawns securely side-by-side on e4 and d4 is an ideal. Heed the word 'securely'. In some openings one side – usually White on account of having the first move – is able to occupy these squares briefly, but is unable to maintain his pawns there.

Pawns at e4/d4 (e5/d5) are strong because they command a line of four vital squares in the enemy position. If one of these pawns is forced to advance, then not only is the number of squares attacked reduced to three, but these are all of one colour, ceding pawn control in the centre of the squares of the opposite colour. This is not to suggest that you must not advance a pawn in the centre beyond the fourth rank. The mobility conferred by pawns on e4/d4 (e5/d5) permits an advance at a time of the player's choosing.

Black's second move above is natural, but he has the choice of good alternatives; for instance, 2 . . . d6; 2 . . . e6; and 2 . . . g6. Each of these leads to distinctive systems, markedly different one from the other. The Sicilian Defence is rich in strategies which accounts in part for its enduring favour.

3.	. . .	cxd4
4.	Nxd4	Nf6
5.	Nc3	d6
6.	Bg5	e6
7.	Qd2	Be7
8.	O–O–O	O–O (94)

WHITE

BLACK

94

Black almost invariably castles on the king's side in the Sicilian but White, depending on the system adopted, may castle on either side. Where he castles on the queen's side, as here, the way is open for both sides to attack the enemy king without restraint.

It is unlikely that an attack with pieces alone can succeed. At least one pawn must be enlisted for the assault. The a/h-pawn is a favourite for this task since when it is exchanged for the opposing b/g-pawn – the usual aim – the rook behind it will come alive with an open file on which to operate.

When the kings face each other on the same side of the board, an attacker who plans a pawn assault must agonize about the consequent weakening of his own king's position. No such problems exist in *(94)*. White will charge with the h-pawn but Black has already an open line on which to operate – the c-file. A sacrifice which sometimes succeeds here is for Black to give up his queen's rook for White's queen's knight to gain advantage in the centre and to disturb the White king position. It is usually a matter of who gets there first, and that means that in situations like this it is unwise to waste time on defensive moves that are likely to be no more than palliatives anyway. Bust or be busted!

A well-tried line in the Sicilian pivots on the capture by Black of a remote pawn. The practice of pawn-grabbing has its advocates and detractors and nowhere more so than in this variation, known as the Poisoned Pawn.

	WHITE	BLACK
1.	e4	c5
2.	Nf3	d6
3.	d4	cxd4
4.	Nxd4	Nf6
5.	Nc3	a6
6.	Bg5	e6
7.	f4	Qb6
8.	Qd2	Qxb2 *(95)*

The theory of this sacrifice is akin to that of most gambits – to displace an enemy man and to hasten development. Here the queen is out of play for at least two moves and White gets an open file for his queen's rook. On the other hand, if Black can hold onto the pawn and develop safely, then the extra man should serve him well later. An example

WHITE   BLACK

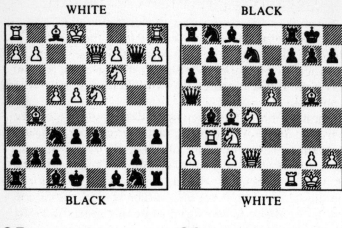

BLACK   WHITE

95   96

of play, which we discussed earlier, where opening strategy is directed towards the end game.

Play might continue:

9.	Rb1	Qa3
10.	e5	dxe5
11.	fxe5	Nfd7
12.	Bc4	Bb4
13.	Rb3	Qa5
14.	0–0	0–0 *(96)*

Black runs for cover while he has time. Latest analysis suggests that the Poisoned Pawn variation is . . . but there, we can safely leave theory to the scholars and screwballs – it will be different tomorrow anyway.

As a general guide, free pawns in the centre are always worth grabbing while gift pawns in the aisles should be judged on the merits of the position.

By contrast to the Sicilian, the mirror defence 1. d4, f5; known as the Dutch, is rarely played. The reason we have already met: Black's pawn advance loosens slightly his king's position. He will not be able to develop quickly enough to castle on the queen's side.

DISARMING THE BISHOP GUARD

A bishop entrenched at b2/g2 or b7/g7 is known as a fianchettoed bishop (fianchetto is a term derived from the Italian, meaning 'side moves'). It affords one of the strongest defensive positions for a castled king, particularly with the help of a knight at c3/f3 or c6/f6 respectively.

There are two common ways of attacking this defence structure. One way is by advancing the a/h-pawn and exchanging it for the b/g-pawn, creating an open rook's file. Here the rook, perhaps joined by the queen or a minor piece, can attack the defence's weak point at a2/h2 or a7/h7 respectively. The other way is to force the exchange of the entrenched bishop. This is achieved by an artificial-looking manoeuvre which is effective only if the attacker has sufficient forces in hand to press the advantage. We can see this action live in our next opening.

	WHITE	BLACK
1.	d4	c5

A safe gambit. If White captured 2. dxc5, Black could retake the pawn at once after 2 . . . Qa5+ but would be unwise to do so since it would leave the queen exposed to attack. The pawn cannot be held, and Black will recapture at leisure. The opening is known as the Benoni.

	WHITE	BLACK
2.	c4	Nf6
3.	d5	e6
4.	Nc3	exd5
5.	cxd5	d6 *(97)*

Black has now the pawn majority on the queen's side in return for a backward pawn. A queen's side majority is an advantage where both sides castle on the king's side because the pawns can be advanced without jeopardizing the king.

In theory, and usually in practice, the majority can eventually be converted into a passed pawn. Face three pawns against two in their starting positions, remove the rest of the men from the board, and prove to yourself that this is so.

Black's backward pawn on d6 however is a permanent

weakness and will have to be guarded constantly. A backward pawn is weak because it cannot be defended by another pawn.

WHITE

BLACK

97

6.	Nf3	g6
7.	Nd2	Bg7
8.	Nc4	

White deploys the knight to a square where it attacks Black's weak pawn: an example of identifying a weakness and setting out methodically to exploit it. White has time to do this because the centre is static.

| 8. | ... | 0–0 |
| 9. | Bf4 | Ne8 |

Black must defend the pawn. A sacrifice is out of the question because, with the pawn on d6 gone, White's d-pawn would be passed.

| 10. | Qd2 *(98)* | |

Now White is in a position to force the exchange of black-squared bishops after 11. Bh6, and any attempt by Black to avert the exchange will work out badly. Black should never consider a move like Bxc3 except in extremity because this would seriously weaken the black squares round his king.

White may be in no hurry to force the exchange. It is sometimes a good idea to lodge a piece at h6 and then to advance the h-pawn. The defence may have trouble stopping the manoeuvre h4, h5, hxg6 when the rook joins in the attack. Without a piece at h6, the advance h4 is often best met by a like move.

WHITE   BLACK

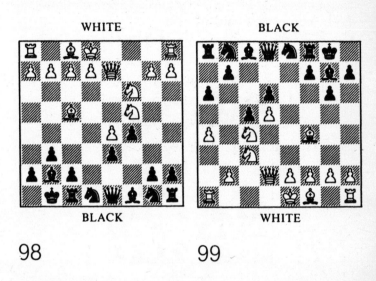

BLACK   WHITE

98   99

Black needs to mobilise the queen's side quickly in order to counter White's threatened attack on the king's side and to capitalise on his pawn majority. He would like to drive away the well-placed knight on c4 but must first prepare the advance.

| 10. | . . . | a6 |

11.   a4 *(99)*

Take in carefully White's reply. This is the usual way of stopping the advance of the b-pawn. (Later on, White might even bring his rook to a3 and then switch it to the other side of the board to join in the attack on the black king – imagination borrows heavily from the unorthodox.)

Suppose White omitted this preventive move and carried on with his plan on the king's side. Continue from *(98)*.

10.	. . .	a6
11.	Bh6	b5

Now White has nowhere to retreat the knight. 12. Ne3 allows 12. . . . Bxh6, and 12. Na3 loses a piece to 12. . . . b4; (it is quite easy, in pursuit of the higher strategy, to overlook tactical trifles – take comfort that even world champions succumb on occasion). The text allows no option; White must take the bishop.

12.	Bxg7	N (or K)xg7
13.	Ne3 *(100)*	

WHITE

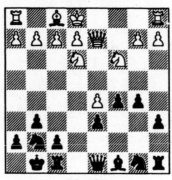

BLACK

100

The position is transformed. Black's pawn majority is making ground, his backward pawn is out of danger and he has an open file for his major pieces. Also, he can switch his queen's rook quickly to the centre via a7.

By contrast, White's set-up is wretched and his prospects rather worse. The king's knight has still not completed his travels and the queen's knight can be chivvied at any time by b4. The advance 13. . . . b4 at once is probably not Black's best even though the knight will have to retreat. If 14. Ne4?, f5; 15. Ng3, f4; and it's that pawn fork again! The drawback of Black's 13th move is that it will allow White's awkward knight back into c4: better to wait until it has moved away before teasing the queen's knight.

A ROBUST DEFENCE

A solid defence system with clear positional aims is the French: 1. e4 e6 *(15)* (page 11). Black allows White to build an impressive pawn centre and then seeks to undermine it to reach a favourable ending. Although the strategy is fairly straightforward, it is liable to be upset by tactical ploys; these facts-of-life that surface unexpectedly in all openings – look back at *(55)* (page 41).

	WHITE	BLACK
1.	e4	e6
2.	d4	d5

The habitual first moves. Now White has significant options; he can exchange pawns, which avoids complications but gives him little advantage, he can bring out his queen's knight to guard the e-pawn, or he can push the e-pawn forward to give a classical French centre formation.

	WHITE	BLACK
3.	e5	c5
4.	c3	Nc6
5.	Nf3	Qb6
6.	Be2 *(101)*	

White might be tempted into 6. Bd3 here in the hope that Black takes the offered pawn: 6 . . . cxd4; 7. cxd4 Nxd4? 8. Nxd4, Qxd4?; 9. Bb5+ and the black queen is feeling unwell *(102)*. However, we have stressed that you should not be seduced by schemes that require your opponent to make a mistake. If after 6. . . . cxd4; 7. cxd4, Black plays quietly 7 . . . Bd7 the threat on the pawn is real and White must either sacrifice or put pride to one side and move the bishop again. Return to *(101)*.

	WHITE	BLACK
6.	. . .	cxd4
7.	cxd4	Nge7

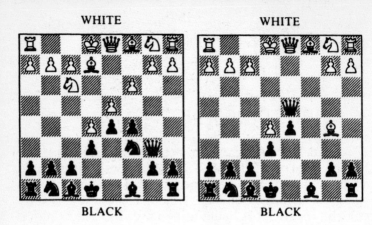

WHITE   WHITE

BLACK   BLACK

101   102

White's d-pawn is weak because it has been deprived of pawn support. Now Black is threatening to win it with 8. . . . Nf5 and if White brings up a third defender (9. Be3) he loses the b-pawn to the queen.

8.	b3	Nf5
9.	Bb2	Bb4+
10.	Kf1	

Otherwise White loses the d-pawn.

10.	. . .	h5 *(103)*

To stop 11. g4 when the knight would have to go to h6 where it would be out of play. If the knight were withdrawn to e7, this would cut off the bishop retreat – these two pieces are inclined to interfere with each other in the French. After 10 . . . Bd7; 11. g4, Nfe7; 12. a3, Ba5; 13. b4 Black loses a piece for two pawns, a poor bargain. (Notice though that White will first have to do something about his undefended bishop. Fortunately, the quarry cannot escape.) White may be planning to move his g-pawn anyway, to allow the king to move up and release the rook. The text (10. . . . h5) discourages this plan. Although White has forfeited the right to castle, he has blunted the attack and now Black's pieces stand awkwardly.

A popular line in the French is shaped by an early pin:

WHITE

BLACK

103

	WHITE	BLACK
1.	e4	e6
2.	d4	d5
3.	Nc3	Bb4

Now White's e-pawn is undefended.

A knight at c3, pinned by a bishop against king or queen, is one of the commonest stratagems in the openings. When executing a pin, you should anticipate an immediate attack on your piece and be clear on the action you intend. To withdraw a bishop along the diagonal on which it arrived is to lose time; avoid it unless your opponent, in driving you away, has somehow weakened his position. The choice is then between capturing the pinned piece or retreating the bishop while maintaining the pin. The latter is often a good plan since although the initial a3 is unlikely to weaken the defender's position significantly and may indeed improve it, the follow-up b4, releasing the pin by shutting out the bishop, may not be wise, especially if the player's king is castled, or intends to seek sanctuary, on that side of the board.

4.	e5	c5
5.	a3 *(104)*	

Now Black has three good options: he can withdraw

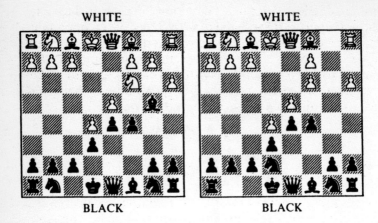

WHITE   WHITE

BLACK   BLACK

104   105

maintaining the pin, exchange the minor pieces or capture on d5 attacking the pinned knight.

5.   ...   **Bxc3+**
6.   **bxc3**   **Ne7** *(105)*

Black is not concerned about 7. dxc5 because the move would collapse White's pawn structure (four pawns on the queen's side and every one isolated) and in any case he will have no difficulty recovering the pawn, as you can easily work out. However, Black does have a few problems. The defences on his king's side are frail and he may have difficulty developing his bishop effectively. The greatest danger however lies in the potential weakness of the black squares, a key positional theme in the French. White's queen's bishop could prove a menace along the a3–f8 diagonal. White's only weakness is his disorganised pawns and for this reason they will be the target of Black's attack. Remember to constantly monitor the board in this way – it is the features, good and bad, of a position that breed ideas.

In the above variation, since Black planned to take off the knight anyway, could he not have done so at once and then moved up the c-pawn? (4. . . . Bxc3+; 5. bxc3, c5.)

What is the difference? It is now White's turn to move

instead of Black's because he has not been obliged to play the unhelpful a3. Do not hurry an exchange; your opponent may waste a move to prompt you to do what you intend anyway! Of course, if he dissolves the pin by removing the pinned piece (by castling, say) then you will have to make an immediate decision on whether you want to exchange or not – the knight may have gone next move.

HOW PIECES PERISH

You saw above how a bishop could be ambushed by pawns. We return to the Ruy Lopez for another example. This is an opening trap called the Noah's Ark on account of its antiquity, not because King Kong has a habit of falling into it.

	WHITE	BLACK
1.	e4	e5
2.	Nf3	Nc6
3.	Bb5	a6
4.	Ba4	d6
5.	d4	b5
6.	Bb3	Nxd4
7.	Nxd4	exd4 *(106)*

Now the pawn must not be taken at once. Best is 8. Bd5.

	WHITE	BLACK
8.	Qxd4?	c5
9.	Qd5	Be6

Defending the mate and the rook simultaneously as well as attacking the queen – what could be called a useful move.

	WHITE	BLACK
10.	Qc6+	Bd7
11.	Qd5	c4 *(107)*

The bishop is lost for two pawns.

It is rare for a knight to be deprived of an escape route unless it walks too far. There is a situation common to a number of openings where, if it strays to the side of the board, it can fall victim to a pawn.

Go back to *(85)* (page 75). In this position, were Black so

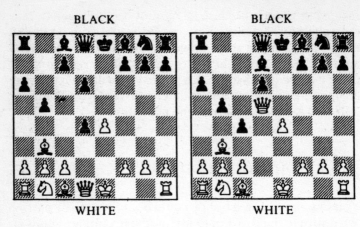

BLACK

BLACK

WHITE   WHITE

106   107

foolish as to take his knight to h5, it would have nowhere to go after the reply g4 *(108)*. Did you say that would weaken White's king's position? True, but you should be willing to suffer considerable damage for the advantage of an extra piece.

It is not only minor pieces that can be lured to destruction on an open board. We have previously seen that incautious forays with the queen can bring condign punishment. Sometimes the penalty can be severe.

WHITE	BLACK
1. d4	c5

The Benoni Defence – remember?

| 2. dxc5 | Qa5+ |
| 3. Nc3 | Qxc5 |

You will recall that this way of recovering the pawn was not recommended.

4. e4	d6
5. Nf3	g6
6. Nd5	Bg7 *(109)*

You would think that the one pawn White cannot now move is the b-pawn because this would expose the rook to the black bishop; but . . .

WHITE BLACK

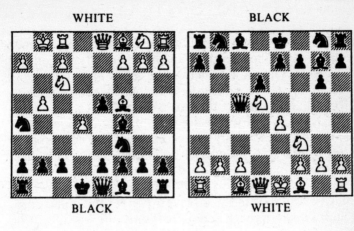

BLACK WHITE

108 109

BLACK

WHITE

110

| 7. | b4! | Qc6 |
| 8. | Bb5! *(110)* | |

Now 8 . . . Qxb5; allows the knight fork 9. Nc7+.

ASSAULT – AND BATTERY

It is hardly to be wondered at that the novice is at times bewildered by the wealth of apparently conflicting advice he receives. He is told to play aggressively and his attack is condemned as premature; he develops his pieces imaginatively and is advised to play natural moves, so makes natural moves and is censured for playing routinely, he's admonished for bringing out his queen and for not doing so.

There are no absolutes of good play, only guidelines. Each position must be judged on its merits alone which is why it is so important to THINK at every move. (Well, at almost every move. Some players ponder the mandatory. If your king is in check and there is only one way of getting out of it, there is no excuse for not moving quickly; you can examine the consequences later.)

Here is an attack that doesn't come off.

	WHITE	BLACK
1.	c4	d6
2.	Nc3	g6
3.	g3	Bg7
4.	Bg2	e5
5.	d3	Ne7 *(111)*

This is an opening we haven't seen before but by now you should be neither surprised nor alarmed by the unfamiliar. Notice that White has command of the central white squares and Black has control of the black. Black's last move indicates that he plans an early f5. Notice that if White were now to pin this piece with Bg5, after 6 . . . h6; he could not withdraw to h4 because of the reply g5 – compare the continuation to *(103)* (page 93). This is an option you surrender when you fianchetto a bishop.

6.	e4	0–0
7.	h4	Nd7
8.	h5	Nf6
9.	hxg6	fxg6 *(112)*

White has conducted a copy-book attack to open the rook's file – but where are the assault troops? Black has

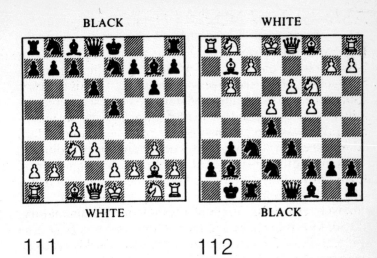

BLACK   WHITE

WHITE   BLACK

111   112

meanwhile got on with his development. The rule when exchanging pawns is to capture towards the centre. Black decided to make an exception here because he wants to open the bishop's file for the rook. A wise decision; if White carries on his plan logically by exchanging the defending bishop he comes to grief; 10. Bh6, Bxh6; 11. Rxh6, Ng4; and now White has both rook and f-pawn attacked and can contemplate an unhappy future.

Before we leave (112), observe that the pawn skeleton creates good outposts for knights for White at d5 and Black at d4 – with one difference; because Black has not moved his c-pawn he can attack d5 at any time.

Here is another attack that fades:

	WHITE	BLACK
1.	e4	d6
2.	d4	g6
3.	Nc3	Bg7
4.	Be3	Nf6
5.	f3	c6

Preparing the advance of the b-pawn.

| 6. | Qd2 | h5 |

Black wants to avoid the exchange of bishops but this is a wasted move since if he castles, White can still force the bishops off with Bh6.

   7. 0–0–0   **b5** *(113)*

Black's pawn formation would have given the old masters heartburn, thus do fashions change.

   8. Nge2   **Qa5**

   9. Nf4   **b4**

An unjustified attack: Black is dangerously behind in development.

  10. Nb1   **Qxa2**

  11. Qxb4 *(114)*

Black's queen is out of play. Further, White is threatening 12. Nc3, Qa1+; 13. Kd2 and any attempt to save the lady by 13. . . . a5 would prove fruitless: 14. Qb3, a4; Qb4 (always keeping guard on the b-pawn) and salvation for Black is out of sight. Of course, Black has a move first but the outlook is bleak.

After 10. Nb1, White is poised to play 11. a3 followed by axb4 for Black's b-pawn is now pinned.

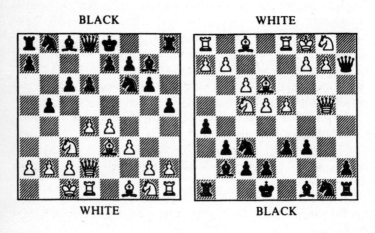

BLACK   WHITE

WHITE   BLACK

113   114

BREAKING THE RULES

One of our two paramount principles is to play towards the centre and we stressed that knight moves to the side of the board are bad. Here is an opening where this, and one or two other maxims, are mutilated in the interests of tactical expediency.

	WHITE	BLACK
1.	**e4**	**d5**

This is known as the Centre Counter; an attempt by Black to get immediate equality. These first moves also occurred in our Cautionary Interlude.

2. exd5

The logical reply. If Black now recaptures with the queen, he will have to move her again after 2. Nc3.

2. ...   Nf6

3. d4

You will find it hard to see why White does not keep the pawn he has won with 3. c4. The reason is that after 3. . . . c6; 4. dxc6, Nxc6; Black has excellent development and White's d-pawn is backward with little chance of advancing to d4. Black has a fine positional game for the pawn sacrificed.

3. ...   Nxd5

4. c4   Nf6

5. Nc3   e5 *(115)*

Black has made three moves with his knight, against the teaching, but White's centre now comes under attack.

6. dxe5   Qxd1+

7. Kxd1

Foregoing the right to castle, but 7. Nxd1 would be a backward step and allow Black a time-gaining check with his bishop.

7. ...   Ng4

Threatening the fork of king and rook as well as the e-pawn.

8. Nh3 *(116)*

The best move to defend the f-pawn. A knight at h3 may

WHITE   WHITE

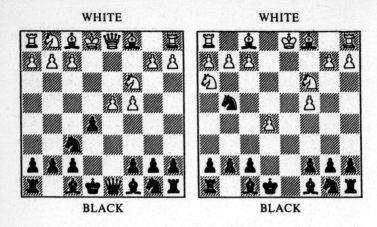

BLACK   BLACK

115   116

later find a comfortable home at f4.

You will not have failed to comment that 8. f4 would simultaneously save the f-pawn and guard the e-pawn but would not prevent the fork. Did you also see that 8. Be3, Nxe3; 9. fxe3 leaves White with a wrecked pawn centre? Less obviously bad is 8. Ke1. The reason this is not good is that White, having forfeited the right to castle, will have difficulty activating his king's rook. If you cannot or do not wish to castle, the king may find safe haven at one of the second-rank squares where it will not impede the development of the rooks onto central files.

White could alternatively have played 8. Ne4 here but after 8. . . . Bf5; he could not develop with 9. Bd3? on account of 9. . . . Bxe4; 10. Bxe4, Nxf2+; followed by 11. . . . Nxe4; and White has lost a piece.

| 8. | . . . | Nxe5 |
| 9. | Nb5 | Na6 (117) |

The same response! Black does not fancy 9. . . . Bd6; 10. c5! (follow through the consequences of this move), nor 9. . . . Kd8; surrendering the right to castle.

| 10. | Bf4 | f6! (118) |

Recall that this is generally a bad move in the opening,

WHITE   BLACK

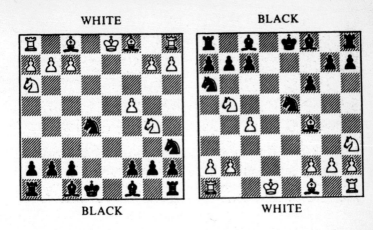

BLACK   WHITE

117   118

particularly true if the enemy queen is still on the board because of the open white diagonals near the king but recall also that a weakness is not a weakness if it cannot be exploited. Now if 11. Bxe5, fxe5; f4 is denied to the king's knight.

Of course, the black knight cannot move without losing the c-pawn while 10 . . . Bd6; 11. Nxd6+, cxd6; would leave Black with a weak d-pawn. The text destroys White's hopes. Now Black will drive the knight back with c6, so White's 9th move was a vain sortie.

A tactical poser that crops up frequently is exemplified in the position. Black is at liberty to play Bxh3, ruining White's pawn formation on the king's side. If this were in front of a castled king, it would probably be a good idea but where it is not is another matter. Here, for example, Black would be ceding the advantage of the two bishops in order to remove a piece that has nowhere useful to go anyway; further, the move would grant White use of the open g-file for his rook. On balance, a bad exchange.

OUTLOOK UNPREDICTABLE

It is not unusual for a stormy opening to settle into a tranquil middle game, nor for a placid start to turn wild.

	WHITE	BLACK
1.	d4	d5
2.	c4	e6
3.	Nc3	c6

A departure from the usual 3. . . . Nf6. This passive-looking move takes away a good square from the knight but Black has planned compensation, as we shall see.

4.	Nf3	Nf6
5.	e3	Nbd7 *(119)*

As peaceful a scene as you could wish to see. Black appears to be putting his efforts into maintaining a pawn at d5 but this can hardly be the limit of his ambitions. Where does he go from here and what does he do about that buried bishop?

WHITE

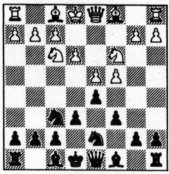

BLACK

119

6.	Bd3	dxc4

We have seen this idea before: Black waits until White moves his king's bishop before capturing the c-pawn; thus forcing the piece to move again.

7.   Bxc4   **b5**

And again! True, Black has a bad pawn formation on the queen's side but this is only temporary. White must counter in the centre before Black gets too much space in which to manoeuvre. Witness the part played by Black's c-pawn.

8.   Bd3   **a6**

Black is preparing the advance 9. . . . . c5; which White cannot stop, opening a fine diagonal for the white-squared bishop.

9.   e4   **c5**

10.   e5   **cxd4**

11.   Nxb5 *(120)*

BLACK

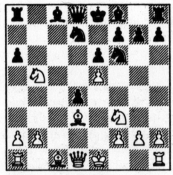

WHITE

120

What will happen now? It's difficult to say because there are a number of plausible continuations. What is certain is that the game is at a critical stage just four moves after the first real contact between the forces.

The wary player expects the unexpected. When your opponent makes a move you have not considered, the first reaction is one of discomfort, if not alarm. It is possible the move is a crusher, but again it is possible that because you did not give it a thought, or your subconscious rejected it, it's a misjudgment. Look beyond the move to the idea behind it. That's good advice for any time, since it is often the coming rather than the immediate which is the danger.

KNIGHTS AND BISHOPS

You have discovered that the most active pieces in the early moves of a game are the knights and bishops.

The text books tell you that these pieces are of approximately equal value, with the bishops preferred in open positions, where they are active, and the knights preferred in closed positions. Two bishops are usually favoured to a bishop and knight and almost always preferred to two knights, as we said earlier.

But these advantages are marginal, and it takes an expert to make use of them.

Bishops and knights may be of equal value but they do their own things. A bishop may move while retaining guard on a square, a knight cannot. A knight always alternates between black and white squares and can reach any square on the board whilst a bishop is restricted to half of them.

Have you noticed that when both sides are developed, it is quite usual for most of the pawns on one side to be on the opposite-coloured squares to those of the other? If, as we suggested, you have been regarding the board as black with white squares and vice versa, you will have picked this up. This is especially true of openings like the French in which the pawn skeletons are locked together. Such formations have bearing on the values of the bishops. Unless the piece is vital for defence, be happy to exchange the bishop that is on the same colour as predominates in your pawn structure, particularly if confined behind it, but try to retain the bishop that is on the predominating colour of your opponent's pawn formation because it will be useful in offence.

We saw an example of an early exchange of bishop for

knight in the Ruy Lopez: 1. e4, e5; 2. Nf3, Nc6; 3. Bb5, a6;
4. Bxc6, dxc6; *(121)*

BLACK

WHITE

121

White has given away the advantage of the two bishops.
What has he got in return?

You are aware of the advantage of a passed pawn. It is
the much-pursued prize in the end game when the vision of
promotion brightens. White is already looking into the
distance. Eventually, by playing d4, he will secure a pawn
advantage on the king's side of 4 to 3 which should in time
yield him a passed pawn.

When White's d-pawn departs, Black will have a queen's
side majority also of 4 – 3. But Black has a doubled pawn on
the c-file; his pawn formation is 'compromised'. Because of
this, Black will not be able to achieve a passed pawn by force
– leave all the pawns on the a-, b- and c-files, remove
everything else from the board, and prove this to your
satisfaction.

This of course is largely theoretical as there are going to
be pieces moving around capturing things for a while yet,
but nevertheless the pawn skeleton is in White's favour.
And in passing, observe the colours of the squares of the

two fixed central pawns – White has exchanged the right bishop.

Another example won't blunt your senses.

	WHITE	BLACK
1.	d4	Nf6
2.	c4	e6
3.	Nc3	Bb4

This is the Nimzo-Indian Defence. Now Black must be prepared to exchange bishop for knight if challenged at once or his move is purposeless.

4.	a3	Bxc3
5.	bxc3 *(122)*	

WHITE   WHITE

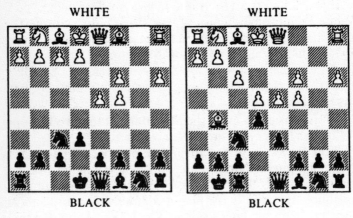

BLACK   BLACK

122   123

White has the two bishops but a slightly weakened pawn structure. Black has a choice of continuations based on different strategical ideas.

5.	...	d6
6.	f3	

With Black's king's bishop departed, this move holds little danger and prepares the advance e4.

6.	...	0–0
7.	e4	e5
8.	Bg5 *(123)*	

This position deserves your attention.

White has built a powerful pawn centre but Black has got his pawns onto black squares so that his bishop has become good whereas White's king's bishop is, at least for the present, bad. Black should under no circumstances consider exd4 since this would not only undouble White's pawns but would render the strong White centre mobile.

White's pin of the knight is designed to embarrass Black. If the bishop is tickled with h6, it will retreat to h4, still keeping the pin. Black will be discouraged from expelling the bishop with g5 since this would weaken his king's position.

If Black had tried the same tactics on the queen's side, White would have been only too happy to continue the pursuit as this would gain a great deal of space at no danger. In fact, in this specific case, it would win a piece for a pawn: 1. d4, Nf6; 2. c4, e6; 3. Nc3, Bb4; 4. a3, Ba5?; 5. b4, Bb6; 6. c5 *(124)*. No harm in another elementary reminder that in pursuit of strategical aims you should not neglect tactical truths!

BLACK

WHITE

124

Another sensible continuation from *(122)* runs:

5.   . . .   c5

In order to fix White's pawn on c4 and perhaps later to attack it.

6.	e3	b6
7.	Bd3	Bb7
8.	f3	Nc6
9.	Ne2 *(125)*	

WHITE

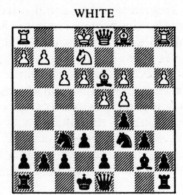

BLACK

125

White has hastened castling and has temporarily immured his queen's bishop in order to give his king's bishop scope. His 8th move prevented occupation of his e4 by a black piece and prepared the pawn move to e4.

Black has solved the problem of developing his queen's bishop. True, the knight masks the bishop's line, but it can move away at any time – and concealed attacks are often the most dangerous.

Having immobilised White's pawn on c4, Black might later attack it with advantage by Na5 and Ba6 coupled perhaps with d5.

A CENTRAL OUTPOST

A fianchettoed bishop puts pressure on the centre and can be a useful support for a knight outpost.

We saw in the last opening *(125)* how White developed his king's knight at e2 in order to stop occupation of his e4 by an enemy piece and to prepare the advance to e4, as in the previous example *(123)*.

The black pawn skeleton *(125)* could equally have been reached from another line against 1. d4: the Queen's Indian Defence. This can come about when White avoids the Nimzo-Indian by bringing out his king's knight first. (Indian defences always involve bringing out bishops sideways: they got their name from the Indian game in which pawns are not allowed an initial two-step advance.)

	WHITE	BLACK
1.	d4	Nf6
2.	c4	e6
3.	Nf3	b6 *(126)*

WHITE

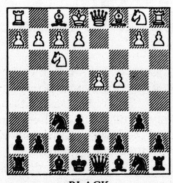

BLACK

126

Can you see Black's strategy? Because White has brought out his king's knight rather than his queen's knight, he cannot play e4 which would give him an advantage in the centre. Black intends to increase his grip on the square with the help of his queen's bishop.

4.	g3	Bb7
5.	Bg2	

One way to deal with a fianchetto on the queen's side is to counter it. We have seen how to deal with a fianchetto on the king's side in *(99)* (page 89).

5.	. . .	Be7
6.	0–0	0–0 *(127)*

WHITE   BLACK

BLACK   WHITE

127   128

What is the significant difference between the two facing bishops? White's is guarded and Black's is not. That is a signal to watch out for tactical coups.

7.	Nc3	Ne4
8.	Qc2	Nxc3

Black always has to worry about this knight being pinned after White moves his king's knight.

9.	Qxc3	f5 *(128)*

Black has strengthened the e4 square and now plans d6, followed by Nd7 and an eventual e5. White also would like to play e4 sometime and can hasten this by moving his knight and exchanging the white-squared bishops.

Instead of taking the knight at once, White might have been tempted to try and exploit Black's unguarded bishop. Take back the last move on each side and play:

9.   Ng5? *(129)*

At first glance, this looks a winner for it threatens mate as well as the undefended bishop. If now 9. . . . Bxg5? 10. Bxb7 and not only is Black's rook under attack but his knight has no escape.

Unfortunately for White, Black has a stunning counter blow: 9 . . . Nxe2+! Now if White replies 10. Qxe2, Black continues 10 . . . Bxg2 and White will end up a piece down however he plays. White 10. Kh1, Bxg2+ is rather worse!

Black has retained his king's bishop, unlike in the exchange variation of the Nimzo-Indian we examined. He could have exchanged it had he wanted. Continue from *(126)*.

4.	g3	Bb7
5.	Bg2	Bb4+
6.	Bd2	Bxd2+
7.	Qxd2 *(130)*	

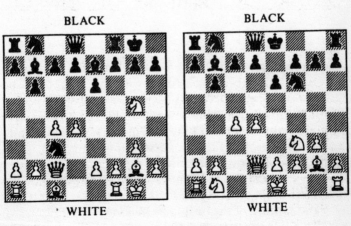

BLACK   BLACK

WHITE   WHITE

129   130

A technicality. White plans a possible d5 so wants his knight at c3 even though it means moving the queen again.

7.	. . .	0–0
8.	Nc3	Ne4
9.	Qc2	

9. Nxe4, Bxe4; allows Black equality as White's attacking chances have disappeared.

9.	. . .	Nxc3?
10.	Ng5! *(131)*	

BLACK

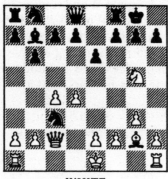

WHITE

131

Now the trap works. Black will lose rook for bishop: 10 . . . Qxg5; 11. Bxb7, Nxe2 (otherwise the knight will be taken for nothing); 12. Qxe2 (12. Kxe2 would allow 12 . . . Nc6 and White has nothing better than 13. Bxc6 on account of the threatened fork of king and queen) Nc6; 13. Bxa8. Notice that Black's 12th move was imperative to avoid losing the rook for nothing. Black now has nothing better than 13 . . . Rxa8; when White is left with the advantage of rook against knight and pawn. Black might be tempted to delay the capture of the bishop by picking up another pawn and threatening the queen with 13 . . . Nxd4. But that would be a mistake as the knight is then undefended (always a danger, remember?) so White could play for example 14. Qe4, simultaneously attacking the knight and defending the bishop to emerge with the bigger advantage of rook against two pawns.

BREAKING THE RULES AGAIN

Contradictions are common in the openings. A good example is Alekhine's Defence where Black brings out a knight, then moves it again – and again. This affront to principles is justified in our equation of give-and-take. Black entices White to advance his centre pawns and then sets about demolishing them – or at least, trying to. The struggle is finely balanced: White has the advantage of space in which to manoeuvre but, as we have seen, advanced pawns can prove weak in the end game – if they don't collapse earlier. Black loses time and gets a cramped position, but that may only be temporary.

	WHITE	BLACK
1.	e4	**Nf6**
2.	e5	**Nd5**
3.	c4	**Nb6**
4.	d4 *(132)*	

As unorthodox an opening as you could wish for! White has a fine centre – but can it be maintained? Compare A Pawn Charge *(88)* (page 79).

4.	. . .	**d6**
5.	**f4**	

After 5. Nf3, Bg4; White will be under some pressure.

5.	. . .	**dxe5**
6.	**fxe5**	**Nc6** *(133)*

Compare *(132)* below. Things are looking a little different now! You can see that Black is threatening N or Qxd4 but White cannot advance the pawn because of Nxe5. That would be a tactical error. What do you think of 7. c5? A positional error. The knight will return to d5 and a Black

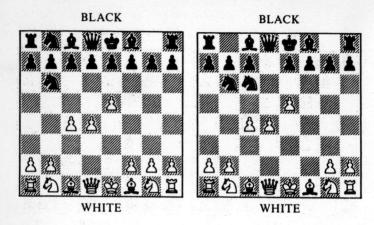

BLACK

BLACK

WHITE

WHITE

132   133

piece will hold the square henceforth; White's centre pawns will be paralysed. At that point, experts would declare the game positionally lost for White.

7.	Be3	Bf5
8.	Nc3	e6
9.	Nf3 *(134)*	

Black must prepare against the advance d5, otherwise White's centre could become overwhelming.

9.	. . .	Bb4
10.	Be2	0–0
11.	0–0 *(135)*	

Lo! Despite the irregular start, we have model development: all the knights and bishops are out and both sides have castled. White still has the powerful pawn centre and now also has an open file for his king's rook. Black must disrupt the centre soon. He might try 11 . . . Bxc3. This would bring two small benefits; it will discourage the advance d5 because it has removed a White guard on that square, and it doubles White's pawns on the c-file where they could become targets of attack.

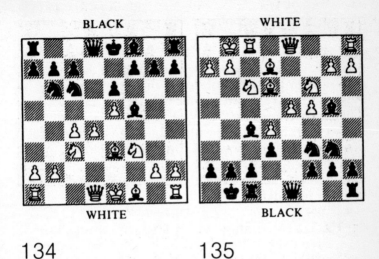

BLACK   WHITE

WHITE   BLACK

134   135

AN EXERCISE IN LOGIC

By way of finale, here is a little game that does not get beyond the opening. It was actually played in a match. White's reasoning, lettered for reference, is given after each Black move. Sometimes the logic is sound, sometimes it is flawed. Can you fault it and suggest improvements for White without sneaking a glance at the subsequent play? If you don't trust yourself, cover the page with a sheet of paper and move it down as you progress.

WHITE	BLACK
1. d4	e5

(a) This offer of a pawn hardly assists Black's development. Anyway, if I don't take it Black gets instant equality in the centre.

| 2. dxe5 | Nc6 |

(b) The pawn is under attack. I can defend it in four ways. 3. f4 weakens the king's position: 3 . . . Bc5; might prove a bit embarrassing. 3. Bf4 breaks a well-honoured opening maxim; develop knights before bishops. 3. Qd5 must be wrong since Black can develop with 3 . . . Nge7 followed, when the queen moves, with Ng6, attacking the pawn a second time. Developing a knight with a step towards castling seems the best.

3. Nf3   Qe7

(c) Black's move must be weak: it brings out the queen too early and in particular obstructs the development of his king's side pieces. However, the pawn is again attacked and if I allow it to be captured my advantage will vanish. There are two ways to defend it, with the queen or the bishop; also I could counter-attack with 4. Bg5 but then after 4. . . . f6; my pawn would disappear and Black would be ahead in development though I would be a pawn up. On balance, I favour a solid defence.

4. Bf4   Qb4+ *(136)*

(d) This is a triple attack, on my king, bishop and b-pawn. Since I don't want to lose a piece for nothing, only two moves can be considered: Qd2 or Bd2. 5. Qd2 must be wrong, because after 5. . . . Qxb2, 6. Qc3 (the only way to save the rook), Bb4 will win the queen for bishop. So I must bring the bishop back – fortunately it is not now needed to guard the pawn.

5. Bd2   Qxb2

(e) True, Black has got his material back and is threatening my rook and e-pawn simultaneously, but I can defend both of these and attack the queen also, forcing her to move once again.

6. Bc3   Bb4

(f) The rook is once more attacked because the bishop is pinned. If I continue 7. Bxb4, Black need not take the rook. He can recapture 7. . . . Nxb4; with the rook still under attack and the only way I can get out of that is to give up a piece by 8. Na3, but even that won't be the end of my troubles. My only resource seems to be Qd2, when I will lose rook for bishop after 7 . . . Qxa1; 8. Bxa1, Bxd2+; however, I shall then have a strong centre pawn, a powerful black-square bishop and the better development – good compensation.

7. Qd2   Bxc3

(g) Of course, if 8. Nxc3, Qxa1+ will leave Black a whole rook ahead.

8. Qxc3 **Qc1 mate** *(137)*

(h) (White's comment here is unrecorded.)

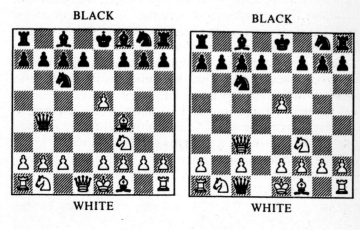

BLACK

BLACK

WHITE

WHITE

136

137

Let's now return to the reasoning and see where White went wrong.

Is (a) correct? Certainly: Black's first move is a gift depriving his king's knight of its best square. No other white move is worth more than a moment's thought.

The logic of (b) is equally valid. The first sentence of (c) is a fair assessment but thereafter the reasoning falters. White could simply develop now with 4. Nc3 and is well in front because of the badly placed queen. The alternative of 4. Bg5 must be evaluated. Black would not continue 4 . . . f6; 5. exf6, but 4 . . . Qb4+; as in the game. Now the bishop is not attacked, allowing White to avoid disaster with 5. Nbd2, but after 5 . . . Qxb2; Black is again threatening the advanced pawn as well as Nb4; so White will lose another pawn at least. Better still might be 5. Bd2, as in the game, but we'll consider that shortly.

Now that the black queen has denied e7 to the king's knight, 4. Qd5 is worth inspection. Because his queen's bishop still guards the b-pawn, White can answer 4 . . . Qb4+, with 5. Nc3 or 5. c3. The knight advance 4 . . . Nb4, threatening both the queen and the fork of king and rook, would be a clear case of a wasted move. White has only to bring the queen back to b3 and the knight would soon be compelled to resume his travels. Black has nothing better than 4 . . . f6 in response to 4. Qd5, when after 5. exf6, Nxf6; the white queen may do best to go home. The extra pawn yields White a decided advantage.

Comment (d) is fair: 5. Bd2 is White's best move here. The logic in (e) is evidently false in the light of subsequent play. White has in fact a perfectly good reply to 5 . . . Qxb2; in 6. Nc3 (138)

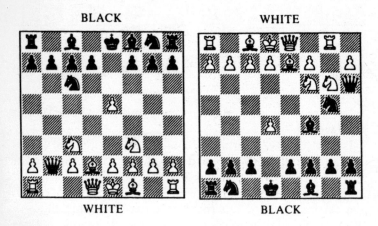

BLACK   WHITE

WHITE   BLACK

138   139

This move is usually the best in situations of this kind. Play might continue: 6 . . . Bb4; 7. Rb1, Qa3; 8. Rb3, Qa5. Does this strike a chord? Look back at (96) (page 86). Now White gets a fine game with 9. a3.

No less difficult for Black is 6 . . . . Nb4; 7. Nd4 (to guard against the knight fork), Bc5 (to break the guard); 8. Rb1, Qa3 (now the knight fork is no longer a threat); 9. Nb3 *(139)*.

Black's bishop is under attack and he will have difficulty extricating his queen. If the bishop goes back to b6 (9 . . . Bb6) White has the pretty 10. Bc1 and Black must give up his knight (10. . . . Nxc2+) to allow the queen to escape. Look also for good white continuations after 9 . . . Be7; or 9 . . . Nc6; or 9 . . . Nxa2. No answers: you are meant to be getting the ideas now!

The retreat 10 . . . Qa6 is met with 11. e3 and the queen has nowhere to go *(140)*. If White plays carelessly 11. e4? Black has 11 . . . Bxf2+ and the queen (but not much else) survives. Black could try desperately 11 . . . Nxa2 and you would reply . . . ?

WHITE

BLACK

140

Comment (f) is all right except for the faulty reasoning in the last sentence.

Comment (g) is correct but the alternative proves fatal. Chess players at all levels are subject to blunders, the result of temporary blindness. There is no known prophylactic but you can stop the disease reaching epidemic proportions by a little self-discipline. One precaution you can take is to draw up a brief check-list which you run through before making each move. Nothing elaborate: something that absorbs just a few seconds of thought.

First, you must identify the main causes of your blunders. These are likely to include overlooking checks, unguarded men, threats – for example, masked attacks – and simple exchanges that destroy a guard. Put them together in a mnemonic and you are in practice.

You could try the doubly-appropriate CHECK, where C stands for Captures, H for Hazards, E for Exposure, C for Centre and K for King. So first you look at the immediate consequences of all possible captures. Then under H you examine for threats, particularly arising from your opponent's last move. Exposure is undefended men – are they in danger? The Centre is a prime concern in the opening – is anything eventful about to happen? Collapse? Rigor mortis? Finally, the king. Look at all possible checks, including those involving sacrifices. You know why checks are important: they severely limit your choice of moves.

That's just an idea for a check-list. You'll be able to think up something better for yourself.

FINAL WORDS ON GOING OUT INTO THE WORLD

That concludes our whistle-stop tour of the openings. A few closing reminders and remarks may be helpful.

For the time being, forget the names of the various openings. Opening fixations (Isn't this the Caro-Kann? Now, what am I meant to do here?) can seriously damage your chess. The reason that some openings have been identified in these pages is to familiarise you with common chess expressions and to impart a little of the flavour of the game. Later you will find it useful to link names to opening play because they encapsulate not only sequences of moves but positional and tactical ideas and, at root, whole systems.

Forget, too, the lines – series of moves – you have been following. They are not representative of the corpus of openings and many you will never see in Master play nor meet in practice. (Awful examples are often the best teachers!) The lines that are worthy of your study you will meet in due course.

It is, as you should now be aware, the *ideas* that are paramount. If you have absorbed them, you will at least know what you are doing in the early stages of a game.

There is no magic formula to alight on the right ideas, but you should try to discipline your reasoning. Constantly scan the board for weaknesses on both sides – unguarded men, badly-placed pieces, damaging checks, vulnerable squares, fractures in pawn skeletons and so on. Collectively, these should suggest a plan of action, and from the plan will come your next move. Don't be in a hurry to force your plan: no game lasts longer than the one you try to win quickly. All that need only take a minute or two; but don't get so besotted with your own plan as to overlook your opponent's schemes. Seek a reason behind each of his moves and watch for any fundamental change in the position (a pawn move is a likely catalyst). If you detect one, revise your plan. A caution: at all times analyse any line of play that appears forced. Not too deep (you'll miscalculate), just a move or two. Your CHECK list should take care of that.

Early on in a game, and preferably before you have completed your development, you should be thinking about where you are going to attack – in the centre or, more commonly because it is easier, on one of the flanks. If your opponent has a decided and permanent advantage in one sector, do not embrace a slow death by attempting to combat it: seek counter-play elsewhere.

And to repeat what was stressed at the start: experiment with every type of opening for this will improve your chess and give you confidence. You will lose a lot of games but thereby acquire a few friends (everyone loves a loser), and anyhow success is on the way.

In these few pages you have discovered something of the richness of chess and how to think constructively about your opening plays. It is to be hoped that you will remember *First Moves* with affection when you come to receive your International Master title.

By the same author
In our Paperfronts series
(Standard paperback size)

BEGIN CHESS

Begin Chess is simple enough to be understood by children. It delves right to the heart of each problem that confronts the beginner, and explains each difficulty with relentless clarity.

Clear and authoritative, this is not just another ordinary book on the game. It is a bombshell of revolutionary ideas that the author has developed over many years of teaching chess to the young and the not so young.

THE RIGHT WAY TO PLAY CHESS

In *The Right Way To Play Chess*, while also covering every aspect of the game, David Pritchard moves on to discuss more advanced ideas. Written chiefly for adults, the book is more comprehensive than *Begin Chess* and contains many extra sample games.

With 224 pages and over 100 illustrations.

During the 20 years that this book has enjoyed *bestseller* status it has been widely praised as the following reviews show:

Chess: 'The best'.
Illustrated London News: 'The best.'
Sunday Times: 'Remarkable'.
The Observer: 'Easy'.
Yorkshire Post: 'Chess without tears'.

BEGIN BACKGAMMON

This book is for the *absolute* beginner. It explains the rules, principles of play, strategy, gambling and, most important of all, the arithmetical probabilities which underlie the throw of two dice. Author Vere Molyneux describes these, rightly, as 'the solid ground on which both tactics and strategy are based'.

PICK OF THE PACK PATIENCE GAMES

Here Jacqueline Harrod describes one hundred of the best patience games, ranging from very simple ones to keep children happy, right up to the most complex ones which demand utmost clarity of thought from intelligent adults! Whatever your standard, here is a plethora of varied, interesting games guaranteed both to relax and, perhaps, to frustrate you.

CARD GAMES PROPERLY EXPLAINED

Develop your 'card sense' using the step-by-step examples in this book, and your skill and understanding of the best card to play will improve no end.

Arnold Marks gives the basic rules for all the best loved card games, including whist, solo, napoleon, contract bridge, auction bridge, poker, brag, cassino, rummy, canasta, cribbage and pontoon.

RIGHT WAY
PUBLISHING POLICY

HOW WE SELECT TITLES

RIGHT WAY consider carefully every deserving manuscript. Where an author is an authority on his subject but an inexperienced writer, we provide first-class editorial help. The standards we set make sure that every **RIGHT WAY** book is practical, easy to understand, concise, informative and delightful to read. Our specialist artists are skilled at creating simple illustrations which augment the text wherever necessary.

CONSISTENT QUALITY

At every reprint our books are updated where appropriate, giving our authors the opportunity to include new information.

FAST DELIVERY

We sell **RIGHT WAY** books to the best bookshops throughout the world. It may be that your bookseller has run out of stock of a particular title. If so, he can order more from us at any time – we have a fine reputation for "same day" despatch, and we supply any order, however small (even a single copy), to any bookseller who has an account with us. We prefer you to buy from your bookseller, as this reminds him of the strong underlying public demand for **RIGHT WAY** books. Readers who live in remote places, or who are housebound, or whose local bookseller is unco-operative, can order direct from us by post.

FREE

If you would like an up-to-date list of all **RIGHT WAY** titles currently available, please send a stamped self-addressed envelope to

ELLIOT RIGHT WAY BOOKS,
KINGSWOOD, SURREY, KT20 6TD, U.K.